Makondo, Guelph

Dobros

I SAW THREE CHINAS

MOLLY PHILLIPS

Orca Book Publishers

Canadian Cataloguing in Publication Data

Phillips, Molly, 1909 -
I saw three Chinas

ISBN 0-920501-43-5

1. China — Description and travel — 1901 - 1948.
2. China — Description and travel — 1949 - 1975.
3. China — Description and travel — 1976 -
4. Phillips, Molly, 1909 - — Journeys — China.
I. Title.
DS712.P54 1990 915.1'04 C90-091119-0

We gratefully acknowledge the financial support of the Government of British Columbia.

Publication assistance provided by the Canada Council.

Orca Book Publishers
P.O. Box 5626, Stn. B
Victoria, B.C.
Canada
V8R 6S4

Cover design by Susan Fergusson.
Typeset by the University of Victoria Students' Society Graphics Shop.
Printed and bound in Canada by Hignell Printing Ltd.

To the memory of my parents, Sidney Frank Ricketts and Ruth Lavinia Briscombe, who began this China odyssey. And to my husband, Richard Gaundry Phillips, who shared some of my China experience.

It should be noted that all Chinese words in the earlier chapters of the book are spelled according to the system in use in the Cantonese dialect at the time. The name for the city of Canton is maintained throughout, although the current name is Guangzhou. Other place names in the sections on modern China conform to the current spelling.

I wish to thank some of my tour friends for a few of the pictures included in the modern section. Because we exchange pictures after a tour, I cannot identify specific persons, but wish to express my appreciation for their generosity in sharing their shots with me.

I should also like to thank Bob Tyrrell and Ann Featherstone of Orca Book Publishers, for their guidance and help in the preparation of this manuscript.

Contents

Foreword

Napoleon is reported to have said, "China is a sleeping giant; let her sleep for when she awakes she will shake the world."

My life has spanned the awakening of this "giant," and circumstances and good fortune have allowed me to observe firsthand the convulsive spasms of this vast and once remote country as it hauled itself into the twentieth century. Born in the closing years of the imperial Ch'ing dynasty, of parents who had gone to China at the turn of the century shortly after the Boxer Rebellion, I was brought up with stories of those years.

The precarious situation leading up to the Revolution of 1911 which overthrew the emperor, sent my parents and me to Canada, but we remained very much in touch with things Chinese. Because of my parents' deep concern for China and the constant presence in our home of members of the Chinese community, issues involving that country were frequently discussed. On Sunday evenings I sometimes accompanied my parents to the Chinese Methodist Mission Church and learned to sing some of the old hymns in Cantonese.

Along with other students I read Pearl Buck's *The Good Earth*, complained about the lack of opportunity for Asiatic students in Canada, deplored foreign "gunboat diplomacy," and agitated for the relinquishing of foreign concessions in China.

I Saw Three Chinas

After graduating from university, I was led, by a strange coincidence, to return to south China during the heyday of Chiang Kai-shek's republican rule and the beginning of the war with Japan. I lived in the centre of Canton, apart from other foreigners except for the three or four staff members with whom I was associated.

After my marriage, I moved to Hong Kong with its 98 percent Chinese population and direct three-hour train service to Canton. I still kept very close ties with China. Moreover, our house servants spoke no English, and my husband taught in an all-Chinese boys' school, which ensured close contact with things Chinese.

When the Second World War caught us on home leave, our family was unable to return to Hong Kong. For the next thirty-five years, I was forced to rely on secondhand information to gain some understanding of events in this troubled land. Returning missionaries brought varied reports, while a few trusted foreigners, permitted to stay in China, were able to give some indication of events. My visit to Japan, Korea, Thailand and Hong Kong in 1964 at least touched the fringes of China. I gazed across the barbed-wire border, longing to cross that line and find out for myself what was really happening.

It was, then, with great satisfaction that in 1974, after four years of applying, I was granted permission to take a group to visit the new China now under Communist rule. Since that time, I have made twenty-two visits to this vast land, during the course of which I have visited over sixty cities and towns in the north, south, east and west.

This is not a travelogue. It is an attempt to see events in China through my own eyes, and to interpret some of its history through personal experience. As a friend once said to me,'' It's the story of someone who has had a love affair with China.''

1. An Engineer's Adventure: Canton, 1904

It was almost midnight as the Hong Kong-to-Canton ferry steamed slowly through the dark. The baggage had been noisily distributed, the third-class passengers below had finally settled down, and, apart from the click of mahjong ivories in one cabin, all movement in first class had ceased. The Chinese businessmen and the few foreigners aboard had retired for the night.

The big sea-going junks rode gently at anchor, and, for the most part, the busy little sampans were at rest. Only the rhythmic thump of the large rear oar indicated a boat creeping through the night. The silhouettes of coastal steamers, ocean liners and British naval boats anchored in double lines along the length of the Hong Kong harbour, were reminders of the seething activity of the day.

For Sidney Ricketts this was no ordinary night trip, no business jaunt to Canton. He sat on the edge of his cabin bunk too excited to sleep. Answering a knock at his door, he accepted a basket proffered him and inspected its contents. A cylindrical teapot stood cosily ensconced in contoured padding. The hot, fragrant tea refreshed him. Then he quietly opened his deck cabin door, and, leaning on the rail, gazed at the distant lights of Hong Kong, "jewel of the Orient." The noisy barter of the day, the shouts of rickshaw coolies, the clatter and clang of streetcars and the grunts of labourers and burden bearers were silenced. The soft cool air of the April night was a relief from the noise and clammy tropical heat to which he was slowly becoming accustomed.

The long trip through the Suez Canal, around the coast of India, the tip of Malay and up the China coast had been a trying journey at times for a young man brought up in the Chiswick District of London. Leaving England in December 1903, Ricketts had celebrated his twenty-first birthday late in January on board ship. After consultations with his head office in Hong Kong and interviews with suitable construction staff, he was now on his way to Canton. He had been commissioned by the firm of Shewan Tomes to build a power station to produce electricity for Canton. It was a historic mission for so young a man, but he looked forward to the challenge.

China at this time was under the rule of the decadent Ch'ing dynasty of the Manchus who had overthrown the Ming emperors in 1644. The Ch'ing, who had held sway in Manchuria for centuries, conquered China proper, but were always considered foreigners and their rule resented. The Ming dynasty had produced an outpouring of cultural and artistic works, but the Manchus, with their often brutal rule, their formality and stifling controls, brought about only stagnation and bitterness. In the nineteenth century, young intellectuals, educated in Europe and America, were eager to implement Western ideas.

But the heavy hand of imperialism still lay on China. The foreigners assumed an air of superiority. Britain, France and the United States controlled customs duties and were joined by Russia, Germany, and Japan in securing territorial concessions. Areas of China were under foreign jurisdiction and subject to the laws of the controlling power.

When Sid Ricketts arrived in Canton, the "foreign devils" were still accorded deferential treatment. Although missionaries lived in small compounds within the city proper, most businessmen, customs officials and diplomats lived on the river island of Shameen, a British concession.

At the turn of the century in Peking, the Ch'ing dynasty was enacting the final scene of a tragicomic farce. Tz'u Hsi, the Empress Dowager, was the power behind the throne. A clever and designing woman, she had been the real ruler of the country for forty years. She had directed the affairs of first her husband, then her son and finally her nephew, consistently opposing all reform. So powerful had she become that, in 1989, when the young emperor issued a number of reform edicts, the Dowager countermanded them all, and no one dared to disobey her. Nevertheless, despite her power, all was not well. Behind a facade of ostentatious splendour and rigid controls, the court moved to its doomsday.

In 1898, the Dowager, pretending to encourage the Self Strengthening Movement, demanded money for a navy. When the money was granted however, the "navy" turned out to be a solid, two-storey marble boat with stained-glass windows and all the comforts of a summer home for the Dowager and her attendants on the lake at the Imperial Summer palace.

Secret societies have always been a part of life in China. During the latter part of the nineteenth century, the strongly nationalistic Boxer Society — known as The Righteous and Harmonious Fists — became powerful. Their chief concern was opposition to the imperialistic activities of the West. As their name implied, they trained in calisthenics and classical Chinese boxing techniques. Imbued with a passionate hatred of foreigners, they fanned the growing resentment against the West's intrusions into their country.

Recurring floods, starvation and foreign intervention in domestic affairs finally roused the Boxers to action, and in June 1900, all "foreign devils" became the target of their terrorist activities. All foreigners were marked for extermination, regardless of their reasons for being in China. Foreign legations in Peking found themselves under siege, military personnel and businessmen were attacked, and unprotected missionaries in outlying settlements suffered brutal assaults. Many people were killed; many families were decimated.

The Empress Dowager, while publicly pretending horror at the Boxers' actions, surreptitiously encouraged them. When she sent troops to deal with the insurgents, the confrontation turned into a friendly get-together, hardly the situation to calm the fears of the foreigners.

The Western Powers were furious. By August, an international force of British, American, French, Russian, Japanese, Austrian and Italian troops had forced the Chinese into submission. Huge indemnities were demanded in payment for the insurrection. More rights were surrendered by the Chinese, and the foreigners made still greater inroads into the land.

It was into the arms of this "restless giant" that Sidney Ricketts sailed that April night of 1904, three years after graduating from the engineering department of Finsbury College, London. His appointment as resident engineer with the China Light and Power Company, a subsidiary of Shewan Tomes, was hardly an impressive one. In 1904, the city of Canton possessed one tiny steam plant of no practical value. Electric lighting was unknown.

As he watched the boat nose its way into the Pearl River estuary, conflicting thoughts filled Rickett's mind. It was up this same river that the early Portuguese traders had sailed to break down the barriers to trade with China. And the same river had carried the merchants who, through the Opium War, had forced China to open up Canton to the notorious trade.

Sidney Ricketts wondered what lay in store for him in this strange land. But being a young man he was full of enthusiasm and optimism. The gentle breeze, the quiet swish of the water against the bow, and a weariness born of excitement and planning finally moved him to his cabin and he fell asleep.

As day broke, thumps, shouts and hurried movements announced the fact that the ship was nearing its destination. By six o'clock, Sid Ricketts was out on deck watching with fascination.

Canton, with three-quarters of a million people, and at that time the country's largest city, was relatively young by Chinese standards. In 1122 B.C., the area surrounding Canton had been designated by the Emperor as barbarian territory, fit habitation for crocodiles and elephants only. Around 300 B.C., as the legend goes, five genii clothed in multi- coloured raiment and bearing stalks of grain, flew on the backs of five rams and settled in what is now Canton. The genii soon left, but before doing so they turned the rams into stone. These statues remain today in the "City of Rams." On the site a settlement grew up, and rice-growing, as predicted by the genii, became a major product of the area. Eventually, in the eleventh century, a six-mile wall, wide enough for five to walk abreast, enclosed the city. That wall remained intact until it was demolished in 1920 and its bricks used for paving new roads.

Ricketts watched the scores of boat people recklessly manoeuvring their single-oared sampans into advantageous positions. Soon yelling coolies prepared to board the ship in search of passengers willing to pay a few cents to have their luggage carried ashore. Sidney was joined at the rail by an American businessman.

"This all new to you?" the stranger asked.

"Yes, I've just arrived," Ricketts replied.

"You'll find it different," chuckled the American. "It's a busy city.

All the goods from the hinterland and the city go up and down the river. There are no real roads anywhere."

As the boat docked, the shouting and jostling, the noise and the confusion increased. The American made ready to depart. "I'm sorry I can't stay," he said as he shook Ricketts' hand. "I see my boy coming on board to pick up my bags. But don't worry. There'll be somebody down to meet you. Good luck."

Ricketts thanked him and stood waiting. Within moments a wiry individual, a long plait of black hair descending from an otherwise bald dome, presented himself.

"You Misser Licketts?" he asked. Ricketts acknowledged the fact.

"Me, Chan," explained the man. "Where your baggage?"

"I have two bags and a trunk in my cabin," said Ricketts, whereupon Chan summoned three men who came rushing up. Choosing one man, Chan assigned him the two suitcases which were promptly attached to each end of a pole carried across the bearer's shoulder. The other two men were told to fetch the trunk. It too was slung on a pole borne on the shoulders of the two. Sidney Ricketts looked with dismay at the ragged, scrawny bearers, and wondered how they would push through the crowds and get his trunk to its destination.

Preceded by Chan, they all edged their way through the throngs to the Customs shed. Here the baggage was cursorily checked by foreign and Chinese inspectors. The men picked up the bags again, and with rhythmic grunts, set off at a trot for their final destination.

"Now we go Shameen," said Chan. "Him belong before-time mud flat. Now velly good place live."

When they arrived at the island in the river, Sidney Ricketts was impressed. Shameen had been, as Chan had indicated, a mud flat, but the British had appropriated it, constructing stone ramparts and rebuilding the small island into a very attractive place. A complete circuit measured only one and a half miles, with two-thirds of the area a British concession and one-third French. Crossing on one of the two bridges guarded by sentries employed by the British, Chan led the way over the fetid canal which separated the island from the main city.

On the island the contrast came as a relief to the dreadful dirt, the dark alleys and the foul-smelling canals that Ricketts had glimpsed along the way. He found himself on a broad avenue lined with huge banyan trees, stately houses and business offices. Small parks and tennis courts offered a retreat from the noise of whining beggars, jeering children, humans groaning under enormous loads and the squalor of a city frequently ravaged by malaria, dysentery and cholera.

Chan led Sidney to an imposing building and up a flight of stairs to a very spacious suite of rooms. Ricketts was delighted. Shameen had been chosen with care so that the outlook down the Pearl River and the frequent breeze off the contour of the opposite bank helped slightly to alleviate the muggy heat.

As they entered the apartment, Chan shouted "Boy." Immediately, the "boy," — a man of indeterminate age — appeared in the doorway. "Boy, this Misser Lickets, Lik Sin Shan, you savvy? You get some tea chop-chop."

"Lik" —力— had been designated as the Chinese surname for Ricketts, as Cantonese was mono-syllabic and had no sound for "r". "Sin Shan," Ricketts learned, was more or less the equivalent of "Mister."

Turning to Ricketts, Chan remarked, "You wantchee something quick-quick, you say 'chop-chop'."

"Chop-chop" was a relative term, as the new arrival was soon to discover. Quick in China seldom meant a speedy performance.

At this moment the door opened and in came a tall Englishman.

"Good morning," said the visitor. "I'm Jim Stewart. You're Sid Ricketts, I presume. Sorry I didn't get down to the boat to meet you, but a big steamer arrived early this morning from Europe with some of the parts of the new engine for the power house. I didn't dare leave them to the care of anyone else. I had to go down and make certain everything was safely stowed."

After tea Stewart took his leave. "We'll have tiffin at my place at twelve o'clock. 'Tiffin,' by the way, is the word used in this part of the world for the mid-day meal."

Starting to unpack his bags, Lik Sin Shan was quickly interrupted by the boy who insisted that it was his job.

"You go look see," said the boy, indicating that the new arrival should investigate his apartment.

The wide verandah overlooked the river. Potted plants, and the wicker chairs arranged to catch any slight breeze, were pleasant and reassuring. Sidney watched with fascination the thousands of small boats on the river: men and women poling sampans loaded with passengers crossing the river, with boxes of goods for delivery, or crates of squawking chickens bound for the market, sampans tied up at banks with washing on a pole protruding from the boat's roof, children climbing on and off the low deck and women cooking over small charcoal braziers in preparation for husbands who might have time between their odd-jobs on land to snatch a noon meal. Out in the stream, the big junks pushed their way between the steamers arriving from Hong Kong or more distant parts, their sails often displaying print and designs indicating they had been made from reclaimed canvas sacks and bales.

For a moment a nostalgic vision of the Thames River near his home crossed Sidney's mind, but it soon vanished as Chan came out onto the verandah saying, "Tomorrow we go see place for you build 'lectic house."

"Why not go this afternoon?" asked the impetuous young man.

Chan looked shocked. "No, no, too hot. Six o'clock morning time more better go."

The impatient Englishman resigned himself to the tempo of the tropics. He would spend the afternoon gathering together his plans and papers, and writing letters to his mother and sisters in England.

2. Life in Canton

At five o'clock the next morning Boy knocked at Sidney Ricketts' bedroom door and entered with a cup of tea.

"Morning, Sin Shan. You have blekfast, then you go look see," he said.

The refreshing tea and cool sponge-down alerted Sidney for the day. As the young man was enjoying a breakfast of tropical fruit and toast, Chan entered the dining room.

"You wantchee chair or you likee walk?" he asked.

"Let's walk," Sidney replied. "More better see," he added, falling into Pidgin English, the strange local lingo which served for communication between foreign businessmen and their Chinese assistants.

One of the passengers on board ship had given him some lessons in Pidgin. He had managed to memorize a few expressions and interpret some basic phrases. He chuckled to himself as he recalled his teacher's recitation of "Little Jack Horner":

Littee Jack Horner
Makee sit inside corner
Chow-chow he Clismas pie;
He put inside t'um,
Hab catchee one plum,
'Hai yah! what one good chilo my!'

Ricketts wondered if he would ever be able to "savvy" this weird language. He was recalled from his musings by Chan.

"Too muchee clowd aloun'," commented Chan, as he pushed his way towards the waterfront. "England man no likee go fitee (quickly). Maybe go man-man (slowly). Hai! wat you tinkee?"

Ricketts got the drift of the question. "Maskee (all right) go man-man. My wantchee look-see plenty tings," he replied.

Chan caught Ricketts' meaning and slowed his pace so the newcomer could look around as they walked and get the feel of the city.

The streets were already full of bustling people. Canton lay behind two massive walls, the outer and inner cities, but between the outer wall and the waterfront was an area which had been the centre of trade for a century or more. The massive warehouses known as "go-down" were situated here, as were the business places of the "compradores." They were the men who handled most of the trade between foreign merchants and the Chinese establishment.

In spite of the crowds there was always passage. People had learned how to move within congested areas, giving way to each other as needed. Followed by a string of noisy, gawking children and the stares of their elders, Ricketts walked with Chan along the waterfront, peering down the little side streets as they went. The streets were actually alleyways, no more than five or six feet wide. The roofs of the single-storeyed buildings met over the centre so that the street was constantly in shadow. Shops lined the streets. On the front of each shop, wide vertical boards attached at right angles advertised the name of the establishment and the goods sold. Already shopkeepers were taking down the boarded fronts in preparation for business.

Following Chan, Ricketts walked along the rough road paralleling the river until they came to a site where ramshackle huts had been levelled. Alongside was a creek cluttered with sampans and small barges loaded with cabbages, two-foot long beans, bok choi, leafy greens, tsit kwa melons, sacks of grain and live pigs from the productive farms of the Pearl River's estuaries. Across the creek a covered market seethed with early morning buyers haggling over prices with the peasants. The noise and confusion alarmed the young Englishman until he realized that the shouts and arguments were all part of market procedure. He stood transfixed, absorbing the sights and sounds: squawking chickens (sold live to assure buyers of a healthy demise), cackling geese protesting their crowded confinement in covered baskets, hawkers proclaiming their wares and haggling housewives loudly denouncing the sellers as scoundrels and offering them half the asking price.

Chan's voice rose above the cacophony of sound. "Master, you come chop-chop see what side you makee 'lectic shop."

Ricketts returned to the purpose of his visit and walked around the area being prepared for construction. Bamboo scaffolding, he was told, would be erected for the workmen who would lay the bricks for the building. The Englishman was at first sceptical of this procedure, but soon found that this was the accepted method used for centuries in Chinese building. Plans called for the creek eventually to be filled in which looked, even to the inexperienced young man, as if it might pose problems.

After inspecting the site, and still trailed by the curious children and idle onlookers, Ricketts returned to his apartment to complete his plans and prepare for the commencement of construction.

In the following weeks, he watched as bamboo poles were tied together with bamboo string and workmen climbed over the sturdy structure as it rose higher and higher. The young Britisher marvelled at the complete absence of nails and hammer and at the strength of the bamboo bindings.

Inside the scaffolding, long trestle tables were set up and the precious engine parts were gradually unpacked and laid out. The manufacture of diesel engines had not yet begun in either England or America. China Light and Power had purchased the third machine that Diesel had built; it had just arrived by sea from Switzerland. Close guard was kept on every screw and bolt, as the loss of any part would mean months of delay in securing replacements by sea from Europe. A bamboo mat roof covered the tables as men were trained to assemble and prepare the engines for installation.

As the building and assembly progressed, Ricketts started to plan the route of the power lines. This was no small task. Custom and prejudice made life for an electrical engineer in China difficult and unpredictable. After long tramps through the narrow alleyways forming the road system of Canton, the young Britisher began to tackle the enormous task of setting up the electric lines which would eventually distribute the power produced at the plant.

This turned out to be much more difficult than expected. Just getting the poles which would support the lines through the streets proved a formidable problem.

"Up-end the poles," Ricketts ordered when the thirty-foot poles came to a turn in the alley. When it was impossible even then to ease the poles through the narrow intersections, the order would go out, "Ask permission to remove the shop signs." Then began endless consultations to secure permission. Shopkeepers regarded the foreigner and his workmen with dismay. Even temporary removal of the signs which advertised their business was viewed with consternation.

"Ask the shopkeeper for permission to put up a pole here," Ricketts said to the linesman in front of a particular shop. But the indignant reply made it obvious that no poles would be permitted in front of the counters.

"Then we must put them in front of the separating walls of the buildings," said Ricketts.

"maskee, t'hat ting no can do," was the response. "Hai yah! belong too muchee bad heart (evil). One piecee devilo haloy (come down) bottom side."

"Not to mention the night robbers," thought the exasperated engineer.

Negotiations amongst the linesman, Ricketts and the shopkeepers, carried on until a site for a pole was finally agreed upon. Then began the malodorous task of removing the stone paving slabs from over the open sewers in order to dig post holes. With no sewage system in the city, slop went into the gutters where it decayed in the humid tropical heat or was flushed away by the frequent heavy rains.

"Must go talkee one piecee tai-pan (head man)," the Chinese supervisor explained. Ricketts groaned inwardly. More palaver, more bargaining.

With no municipal government, each local ward had to be dealt with on an individual basis. Each block had its own committee and negotiations had to be carried on with the head man. A separate contract would be agreed upon with each block. The usual arrangement was for a flat rate per bulb. The main switch was thrown on at the power house at dusk; there was no power during the day.

At sundown, road blocks, consisting of closely set posts dropped into holes, were erected and the area patrolled by the street guards. At that time families gathered for their evening meal and traffic virtually ceased. Guards patrolled from roof to roof along a catwalk which ran the length of the street, sounding a gong each hour to demonstrate their vigilance. Poverty and unemployment drove many to thievery. A length of wire or string, a discarded cigarette butt, a screw or nail, a piece of paper, bottles, rags and garbage were all booty for night thieves. A careless householder who inadvertently left an item out to dry or air would never see it again.

No one was allowed on the catwalk except the guards, although the rooftop sidewalks were ideal for line inspections, particularly as they gave access to homes. After a time Ricketts was able to inspire sufficient trust to be permitted to use the walks. But no one was allowed to accompany him, so he had to conduct his inspections entirely on his own.

One day a linesman came looking for Ricketts. "Sin Shan," he reported, "Blong trouble power house, I no savvy why."

"I'll go along the catwalk and see if I can find the cause," said Ricketts.

He was not long in discovering the source of the problem. To his astonishment, the 2,000-volt power line suddenly disappeared through a new brick wall built by an enterprising man who had dared to risk putting up a second storey. It never occurred to the man to ask for the lines to be rerouted; in fact, they could be very useful in his house for hanging out the wash. Ricketts directed his man to cut the lines and reroute them outside and over the building.

Instructions were then issued to inhabitants not to use power lines for their own purposes. But well-slung lines were much too useful to remain unused. The family wash or blankets and mattresses to be aired were frequently hung on high voltage cables. Because insulation was good and power was turned off during the day, many industrious servants were saved from instant annihilation.

Still, this disrespect for electricity was not without its tragic side. One day Ricketts saw a large crowd gathered. He hurried to the scene of shouting and commotion.

"What's the trouble?" Ricketts asked as he saw a man lying on the ground, his inert body being beaten with a rubber boot.

After a quick consultation with members of the crowd, the head linesman explained that the man had touched some live wires and had been electrocuted.

"Him savvy my no makee tlouble when hab got lubber boot and lubber glove. Him tink lubber boot catchee 'lectic devil," he explained.

Ricketts pushed his way into the crowd and applied artificial respiration. Just when the victim showed signs of revival, a tropical storm suddenly broke. "Carry him room-side," ordered Ricketts. The linesman turned to the storekeeper to ask permission for the man to be carried into the shop.

"No can come this side. Dielo (dead) body no plopa--belong too muchee bad luck."

Ricketts grabbed some nearby boards and improvised a stretcher. "Faitee wylo (quickly go) power house," he ordered. The linesman and crew picked up the burden. But the narrow streets made the carrying of a stretcher very difficult and twice the body slipped off when the workers negotiated the corners. As soon as the group arrived at the station, Ricketts began treatment again, but the victim's strength was gone and all efforts to revive him proved futile.

Power poles carried wires to ground but wire was too useful simply to hang from a pole when it could be used to mend a vegetable basket. Consequently these wires were frequently snipped off to head height. On one occasion the linesman came to investigate a small crowd who were laughing and shouting. As he approached them, he heard one coolie betting another that he wouldn't dare touch the end of a live wire dangling above his head. Before he could be stopped the daredevil had climbed on a rock and grasped the wire. The gambler won the bet but his heirs failed to collect.

The coming of electricity to Canton lead to other more light-hearted escapades. At dusk one evening, loud shouts of "Fire! Fire!" were heard. Sid Ricketts stepped out on to his verandah and saw light suffusing the sky. He sent Boy out to investigate. The servant came back grinning.

"Him fire boy run chop-chop" he announced gleefully. "No b'long fire, Massa. One piecee big light makee all same fire."

It was as Ricketts had suspected. The first arc lamp installed outside a public building had thrown its light into the darkening sky and the fire department had come on the run.

But the novelty did not last long. Electric lighting became so popular that soon China Light and Power could not keep pace with demand. By

1905, officialdom was convinced of the benefits and the Chinese Viceroy of South China ordered his "yamen" — the compound of the official residence of the local governor — to be wired.

As soon as the initial installations for the city were completed, the company set out to electrify the home of the Viceroy and his more than three hundred wives and concubines. Needless to say this was a very delicate task. It was imperative that none of the women be seen by the workmen. Ricketts and his crew had to beware of intruding upon the Viceroy's harem, particularly the painted favourites in their small screened rooms. But feminine curiosity triumphed. Heads peeped around corners and on one occasion, when Ricketts back-tracked to do some rechecking, he came upon thirty gaping females who screamed and ran.

Shortly after the installation was completed, the city had a festival for which a large decorated gateway was erected across the street leading to the Viceroy's home. Since the electric wires were in the way, six of them were tied together by the gate builders and yanked to one side. Ricketts was notified by his men.

"Take the crew and cut a hole through the gateway and free the lines," he ordered.

But the men soon returned. "Allo man say no can do," they reported.

"Who man?"

"Allo man. Him makee dancee, sing-song, chow-chow street-side. Him kick up one piecee big bobbely (fuss)."

Ricketts called over one of his crew, asking him to take a written message to the Viceroy.

"I regret," the message stated, "that the yamen lights will not be turned on tonight. The plans for the festivities have interfered with transmission."

Before long the linesman returned triumphantly, escorted by a vice-regal guard detailed by the Viceroy to protect the workmen while they cut a hole in the gateway.

As electricity became more and more popular and its use more widespread, the demand for power led to the decision to build a reinforced concrete building — a new type of construction in that day — to house the generating plant. The Chinese authorities began filling in the creek running beside the power company property, so the reclaimed land could be sold for the expansion. No sooner had work begun, however, than the thousands of people who lived on the water furiously objected. The creek was the equivalent of a commercial parking lot. Here all the small junks and sampans from the countryside tied up to unload the enormous baskets of vegetables which moved in a steady stream to the huge market nearby. The wicked foreigners were blamed for the decision to reclaim the creek, and feeling ran high.

And the problems did not end there. Forty-five-foot piles were being driven into the waterfront for concrete footings for the new building. Pile-driving machinery was all hand operated with trip hammers weighing about three-quarters of a ton. When the tidal action of the nearby ocean raised the level of water in the river, sampans would tie up to the piles already driven.

One day, Sid Ricketts was sitting in his office when a brick crashed through the window. Jumping to his feet, he looked out to see a large crowd angrily demonstrating in the marketplace facing the power house. Leading the insurgents was an old lady who, along with her supporters, was harrying the pile-driving crew and machinists with rocks and bricks. The young engineer immediately saw the grave danger of the situation. The mechanics were assembling the power generating machinery out in the open under a matted roof while waiting for the building to be erected. If the crowd surged into the work area, there was great danger of losing machine parts, replaceable only from Europe after long weeks of shipment by sea.

"Man the fire pumps," ordered Ricketts. The power house had laid water mains to a few adjoining streets and acted as a fire extinguishing company. The power house crew turned on a light stream of water. The milling crowd was soaked. They retreated to the market. Ricketts immediately invited the head man of the market to tea and asked him why there had been an uproar.

"Olo lady Wang velly angly. Him scoldee bad," was his explanation. "Allo man makee big bobbely. Hai yah! You coolie man hab makee sinkee him sampan."

Ricketts discovered that a trip hammer had broken loose from a pile-driver and plunged through the bottom of the boat belonging to the peasant woman who had led the attack.

Ricketts invited the old lady to come in and discuss the problem with him. When she appeared, he apologized for the accident and offered to pay her forty dollars to replace her boat. Mrs. Wang beamed and bowed in appreciation. Forty dollars would easily pay for two boats similar to the one she had lost.

Ricketts accompanied the old lady and the head man to the marketplace where the crowd greeted him with approval. They chatted and laughed about their wetting, which on a hot summer day was not a serious matter.

Sidney Ricketts was grateful, after these demanding days, to be able to retire to his own premises. The large, airy buildings with their wide verandas were built on Shameen to house members of the English-speaking community. The homes were islands of physical and social relaxation. Friendly gatherings, usually in the form of dinner parties, enlivened the restricted life of the residents.

Servants would often appear to help serve table at a meal to which their employer was invited. If the party was unusually large, it was not unknown for a guest to see his silverware or plates gracing the table to augment the host's cutlery and dinnerware. The servant network was very efficient.

On one occasion, Sid Ricketts was invited to dinner by the American Consul and his wife. When the servants came around with the vegetables, the young Englishman declined corn on the cob. He had never seen it before.

Noting his refusal, the Consul's wife said, "Mr. Ricketts, do have some corn. I think you have probably refused it because you don't know what to do with it."

Ricketts admitted this was true.

"We've had it imported from the States as we're very fond of it," explained his hostess. "Do take a cob and I'll show you how to eat it." From that time on Sid Ricketts was a convert and developed a keen taste for corn on the cob.

On occasion, servant practices were somewhat bizarre. One of Ricketts' friends remonstrated with his cook for using his master's sock as a food strainer.

"No matter," countered the servant. "Sock no b'long clean one."

Young Britishers soon learned to develop sports within the confines of the little island, and grass hockey was a favourite pastime.

Periodically, the men would go down to Hong Kong to play. Their keenest opponents were the East Indian Police Grass Hockey Team.

The police hierarchy in Hong Kong consisted of British officers in control, the Sikhs serving them and the Chinese police on the beat. The Sikhs, trained in India by the British, were keen hockey players who somewhat unnerved the new British members by playing barefoot. But the British soon learned that hard balls and sticks did not daunt the Indians, and games, as a result, were fast and challenging.

Cricket, of course, was also introduced by the British and served as an alternative sport.

By 1906, the expansion of the electric company demanded more foreign staff and three more Britishers joined Ricketts at the plant. Then in 1908, the Chinese government decided to take over the power house, and, after negotiating with the company, the transfer was concluded. The three new men stayed with the plant to assist in its operation, while Sid Ricketts was called to open and manage a machinery department for Shewan Tomes, his firm in Hong Kong.

Meanwhile, on the political front, pressure on the corrupt and decadent Manchus continued. Revolutionaries led by Dr. Sun Yat-sen demanded reform; less radical elements suggested a constitutional monarchy. The Empress Dowager never intended to accept any democratic changes. After vetoing a number of reforms which the young Emperor had promulgated, however, she agreed finally to an "Outline of Constitution," which in actuality offered no benefits to the people. The outline also required nine years of preparation and reorganization. At seventy-three, the Dowager was making certain that delay would insure her continuous reign.

Three months later, however, she became seriously ill and died on November 15, 1908. Imprudently the thirty-seven year old Emperor had rejoiced over the Dowager's imminent death. He died the preceding day. A well-substantiated rumour circulated that the Dowager poisoned him so that he could not gloat over her death.

Tz'u Hsi had chosen her three year old grandnephew, Pu Yi, as successor, but with her demise the little emperor's father, Prince Chun, became regent and posed as a supporter of democratic reform. Throughout 1909 and 1910, he received delegation after delegation from the provinces who urged him to establish a parliament. But Chun had no intention of relinquishing power. His sole concession in the end was to announce that the period of preparation and reorganization would be reduced from nine to six years.

The people of China were disillusioned. They saw no hope for reform under the Ch'ing dynasty of the Manchus who, after nearly three hundred years of rule, were still considered foreigners. Popular support began to swing towards the revolutionary forces.

3. A Teacher Finds Romance

The wind whipped through the bamboo trees and rattled the windows. The temperature, which had been in the high eighties a few hours earlier, was dropping rapidly.

On that January day in 1905, the missionaries in the Chinese language school in Canton were beginning to shiver. A few, warned of the sudden winter change by veterans who felt the early morning wind shift, had come prepared with light sweaters. The greenhorns envied them their foresight and marvelled how morning perspiration could turn damp clothes cold and clammy by afternoon.

The airy classrooms with twelve-foot ceilings were built for tropical heat. Loosely fitted french doors and draughty windows admitted the tail end of Siberian winds which spent themselves as they crossed the Tropic of Cancer just north of Canton.

Ignoring the changing weather, the class continued to recite the various tones of Cantonese. As Ruth Briscombe joined in, she was fascinated by the sing-song quality of the Cantonese language.

"T'in, t'in, t'in," recited the students in a high tone level, with even, rising and departing tones.

"T'in, t'in, t'in," they continued with the same inflections in a lower voice range. For words ending in k, p or t, they intoned three levels "tit, tit, tit."

During the autumn of 1904, some eight months after Sidney Ricketts had arrived in Canton, Ruth Briscombe had been appointed to South China by the English Wesleyan Methodist Mission Board. A graduate of the London University class of 1900, she had taught in England for four years before being posted to educational work in the mission field. Immediately upon arrival, she was assigned to the usual two years of language study.

Having grasped the basic concept that the same word spoken in a different tone and inflection had a different meaning, she was now struggling with the thousands of words that had to be memorized. She had joined the laughter which followed the mission supervisor's caution to new recruits.

"Get those tones right," he had emphasized. "One of your colleagues who wasn't blessed with much tonal sense got himself into difficulties. When he was called upon to preach his first sermon in Chinese he chose as his topic 'The Lord's Prayer.' He began by saying, as he thought, 'I have a Father, you have a Father, and our Father is in Heaven.' Now you have learned that the word for father is foo, and for heaven is t'in. But do you remember what foo and t'in mean?"

A ripple of laughter had increased as one by one the students grasped the mistake.

"Yes, it was rather difficult for the congregation," said the supervisor, "when they heard the minister saying, 'I have trousers, you have trousers, and our trousers are in the field.'"

The class groped its way through basic characters. Speaking Chinese was one thing; reading was another. The first Chinese characters were logical pictures of the real thing. For example, a field was —田— and a man was —人—. But as language developed, characters became complicated and word groups were necessary to express ideas.

Despite the difficulties, Ruth Briscombe persevered. By the end of her two years of study she showed a decided aptitude for the language. She was ready to begin her work supervising mission schools and visiting in the homes.

In China, schooling was neither free nor compulsory and was largely for the middle- and upper-class families. Ruth was happy her church could provide schooling for many children who would not otherwise have had an opportunity to study, particularly the girls for whom an education was considered unnecessary. She became used to seeing the fortunate girls who were permitted by the family to attend school being conveyed there in covered sedan chairs or accompanied by woman servants who carried the students' books and umbrellas. Co-ed classes did not exist except in the case of very young boys who were accepted in the first grades of girls' schools.

Walking the narrow alleys, lifting her skirts to avoid the filth, she would listen for the sounds of school life. The loud sing-song recitation would penetrate the street clatter, and Miss Briscombe would know that she was approaching one of her schools.

When the English supervisor entered, the girls would stand and demonstrate their rote-learning, turning their backs on the teacher and reciting in loud voices the lessons they had learned. Bible study would follow, led by the missionary and often assisted by a native "Bible woman," whom the missionary was training to assist her in her school and home visiting.

Arriving one day at a home, Ruth Briscombe found a little girl sobbing in pain. Her tiny feet had just had the bindings tightened so that the toes were turned firmly under. Eventually only a stump of a foot would remain.

"You must not bind her feet," Miss Briscombe implored. "It is cruel and unnecessary."

"My daughter is not a servant or a peasant," the mother replied. "She must have three-inch golden lily feet or we will not find a good husband for her."

"Look," said the English teacher drawing a tiny 2 1/2 inch shoe from her bag. "This shoe belonged to the wife of an official in this city. She gave it to me last week because she has unbound her feet. Unbinding is just as painful as binding, but she says foot binding is not good for Chinese women. Her husband has given her permission to unbind her feet. She wants me to tell the mothers of little girls."

The mother looked sceptically at the tiny shoe. "No, my husband would not permit it," she said. "My daughter's husband would not be able to control her. She might even run away."

Miss Briscombe sighed. It would take time, but slowly foot binding was being discontinued, particularly in South China where modern ideas were more readily accepted.

But she had a happy thought. June was the month when the lichee ripened. Their tough red skins looked almost like huge strawberries, but the luscious white fruit within tasted delightfully refreshing. She had seen the cook carrying bunches of the fruit home from market that morning and was eagerly anticipating the first lichee of the season.

That afternoon she walked thoughtfully back to Tsang Sha, the area in Canton where the Wesleyan Mission compound was situated. She was grateful for the cup of tea and the cake which always awaited the staff at four o'clock. The day was hot and muggy, and her long skirts clung to her legs. It would be a relief when the servant woman brought the buckets of bath water and she could wash away the dust and perspiration. June was always a hot month, and if a typhoon was off the south coast, the atmosphere was oppressive.

Canton, she thought, offered so many new foods, particularly tropical fruits that she had never tasted before: persimmons, pomegranates, papayas, mangosteen, pomelos, mangoes, pineapples, star fruit and, of course, all the many varieties of oranges and bananas. And she knew peaches had always been a favourite in China. Legends and folk tales spoke of peaches as the fruit of the emperors and the symbol of immortality. True, there were foods she missed, but there were many more which she found new and flavourful.

As she relaxed in the comfort of a cool rattan chair waiting for the other missionaries to arrive for tea, Ruth wondered about the rumours she had heard of discontent and talk of revolutionary new ideas. Students, often educated in mission schools, were now going overseas for further training. Many were returning with radical new ideas.

Ruth smiled to herself. Hadn't she just been proposing a radical new idea to a mother of a young girl? Wasn't giving up foot binding a revolutionary change in tradition?

These unsettling thoughts faded, as several of her colleagues came in and sat down wearily. The day began early in this tropical land, and by late afternoon tired staff were glad to sit for a time and enjoy a refreshing cup of tea and a little time to chat with one another.

"I hear there's been another uprising in the province," commented one of the men.

"They're happening all over the country," added another.

"The Min-pao (People's Tribune) seems to be stirring up both the intellectuals and some of the more progressive army officers."

"I wonder if Sun Yat-sen is ever going to be able to unite all the dissenters and achieve any change?" Ruth wondered.

"It's going to take a mighty effort to move the heavy hand of imperial power," said one of the men as he rose. "Meanwhile I have to prepare a sermon for Sunday night."

The group laughed. "Yes, I'd forgotten," someone remarked. "It's your turn to take the service, isn't it?"

Canton had a fair-sized missionary population as well as a considerable business community of foreigners. Although traditional class distinctions tended to keep the groups socially segregated, the Sunday evening English service at the Union Church on Shameen brought together those interested in meeting for worship.

It was here that Sidney Ricketts and Ruth Briscombe first became acquainted. It was difficult for them to see each other very often, however. Men and women were never seen on the street together in China, nor did they walk in one another's company. Naturally the missionaries took great pains to avoid indiscreet appearances that would offend the Chinese.

On one occasion, Ruth was trudging home through a foul-smelling lane when Sidney approached, carried in his sedan chair by three bearers. It was with the greatest reluctance and embarrassment that he passed Miss Briscombe without the slightest acknowledgment, knowing that this was the only acceptable procedure.

But life was not all work and study. Several missions had compounds with limited grounds for sports, which frequently included tennis courts. Ruth Briscombe loved to play tennis. In spite of billowing ankle-length skirts, the women of the day somehow managed to enjoy the game. The tennis courts became the centre of social gatherings. Tea and tennis brought together the English-speaking communities, especially the missionaries, who were scattered in various parts of the city. Ruth and Sidney were able to enjoy one another's company at these compounds, uninhibited by the restrictions of Chinese society.

Across the river from Shameen there was a very pleasant mission compound. On the spacious grounds and around their staff dinner table, busy missionaries and compatible business people were occasionally able to relax and become better acquainted.

As their romance developed, Ruth and Sidney were often invited out to dinner, particularly by Rev. and Mrs. Davis of the New Zealand Presbyterian Mission who opened their home to them, allowing the young couple to become better acquainted. Finally, early in 1908, they became engaged. At this point Miss Briscombe was able to make arrangements to be released from her mission contract.

The wedding was set for October 29, 1908 — a welcome social event in the community. Chinese tailors, adept at copying Western clothes from pictures, fashioned a beautiful white wedding dress. Complete with bridal veil and flowers, Ruth presented a charming picture as she and Sidney were married in the Tsang Sha Christian Church where she had worked.

Friends gathered in the grounds of the Wesleyan Methodist Mission nearby for a garden reception in the pleasant weather of late October. In the evening the couple left by night boat for Hong Kong and a honeymoon in a mountain resort near Shanghai.

As Sidney Ricketts was now stationed in Hong Kong, the newly-weds took up residence in Kowloon, the New Territories leased by the British on the mainland opposite the island colony of Hong Kong.

With servants to take care of all the household duties, the young Mrs. Ricketts found time to assist in the extensive mission work in Hong Kong. As Sidney was an Anglican by upbringing, the couple attended the Kowloon Anglican Church which catered to the many foreigners in the community.

In October, 1909, Ruth was due to deliver her first child. On October 14, Hong Kong was anticipating a typhoon. The big black ball, a weather indicator, had been hoisted on the waterfront tower for several days, warning that a typhoon was moving in from the south. Terrified by the memory of the unannounced typhoon which had devastated the colony the previous year, people were apprehensive. After that disaster, five thousand bodies had been recovered from the harbour. Thousands had also been lost at sea, including all the staff and students of the theological college who had been on a sea cruise. Lightly anchored merchant ships had been driven up on the waterfront streets. A misunderstanding between the Philippine and Hong Kong weather stations had led to a failure to report the advancing typhoon and Hong Kong had been caught unawares. This time no one wanted to be unprepared.

As Sid Ricketts sat at the desk in his Hong Kong office, he watched the ball closely. The number one ball, which was a general warning, had changed. The balls indicating direction and proximity of the storm had gone up. Ricketts cleared his desk and decided to head for the Star Ferry which he could see from his window. The ferry was already battling a stormy sea as it made the ten minute crossing from the island of Hong Kong to the mainland settlement of Kowloon.

Sid glanced at the calendar — October 14. He hoped that Ruth would not choose this day to deliver their child. He ran for the ferry as the number nine ball went up, signalling the imminent arrival of the storm. He caught the last ferry crossing the harbour. Warships, liners and merchant ships had thrown out all their anchors and were straining full steam into the wind, battling to stay in their assigned moorings in the harbour. All small boats had long since sought refuge in typhoon shelters and were giddily tossing on the troubled waters.

With a final plunge, the ferry bumped along the Kowloon wharf and disgorged its passengers. Everyone ran for cover. No rickshaws were in sight. The few buses still operating were taking their last load as they headed for their parking enclosures, their drivers hoping to get home before the number ten signal went up and the full force of the typhoon hit the colony.

Ricketts, holding his hat close to his chest, fought the powerful wind and finally arrived at the door of his home in the residential area. He was glad to be out of the shopping area as store signs were creaking, trees were swaying and debris was swirling down the street.

No sooner was he in the door, when the servant woman greeted him. "Missee, chop-chop have baby," she announced.

"Is the doctor here?" demanded the expectant father in panic.

"Nurse come. Boy go fetch doctor."

Ricketts dashed up the stairs and found his wife well advanced in labour. A British nurse assured him all was well. Almost immediately came the welcome sound of the doctor's arrival just as the final number ten signal went up.

With the typhoon raging outside, baby Mary made her entrance into the turbulent world. Her father in later years jokingly remarked, "She was born in the middle of a typhoon and she's been living in one ever since."

A nurse-amah was employed to help with the care of the new baby. "Ma-lei" she said approvingly. "Good name, Ma-lei." With no "r" in the Cantonese dialect, Mary became Ma-lei, and inevitably Molly became my name.

Amah was absolutely devoted to the new baby and watched over her with the greatest care. While Mother fed the baby, the wash-amah gathered up all the daily laundry, and baby-amah prepared the bath. Water was boiled in large cans and then cooled to the right temperature, and Ma-lei was lovingly bathed and lightly dressed. A large English pram had been purchased by my parents, and amah proudly took baby for a walk each day. In the park nearby other amahs gathered with their charges, each acclaiming the superiority of their protege.

As I grew, amah and my parents watched over me carefully. No child was allowed to crawl on the floor for fear of contamination, but there were always loving arms ready to dangle me or assist me to crawl on a clean bamboo mat or a settee. In the short weeks of winter when I was a toddler, I was often dressed in a warm padded Chinese suit that was so comfortable in the airy, high-ceilinged rooms.

As I began to talk, I adopted both English and Chinese words, sometimes both. For years I always referred to a horse as "horsey-ma", combining both languages. My amah was a refined woman and I learned good Chinese from her with ease. As Chinese is mono-syllabic, and children are natural imitators, youngsters find it easy to pronounce and inflections are no problem. Mother and Father spoke to me in English, so I became bilingual at an early age.

While life appeared to be flourishing placidly in Hong Kong, events in China were leading to a major crisis that would change the course of our family life.

China was in ferment. Wider vistas were opening for some of the young Chinese men. The advantages of a foreign education were now recognized, and many students, often educated in mission schools, were sent by their families to study overseas in Western universities. Even greater numbers of young men congregated in the rapidly developing universities of Japan, where Japanese support for a Pan-Asia movement gave encouragement to the radically-oriented students. Technological and scientific training and the stimulation of new ideas, soon began to affect the course of Chinese history.

Sun Yat-sen, a Christian graduate of a mission school in Canton, was one such student. After studying overseas and acquiring a medical degree, he began to organize students and radical groups into a revolutionary force. Meeting with restless and discontented students and secret societies, chiefly in Honolulu and Great Britain, he formulated a plan of action. His famous "Three Principles of the People" outlined the development of a nationalism designed to gain national freedom, establish a democratic system, and raise the standard of living of the masses.

Kidnapped while visiting in London in 1896 and then released, Sun had become a well-known world figure. When the Boxer Rebellion erupted in 1900, the subsequent internal disorder created more dissatisfaction. An international army suppressed the Boxers and China was humiliated by the terms of a treaty forced on her. Her subjugation encouraged those who could no longer believe in a constitutional monarchy. Many began to rally round Sun to plan revolution and the establishment of a republic.

Supported by students, the progressive intelligentsia and the more enlightened military officers, the Chinese United League, with Sun Yat-sen as chairman, was founded in 1905. It was a major step in the move to republicanism.

Meanwhile, rapid expansion began to take place in China. Machinery, electrical equipment and heavy materials were all in demand as a railway craze seized the country. Provinces planned railway lines, foreigners bought into railway companies, and Hong Kong financed a multi-million-dollar loan. The Ch'ing government, wishing to keep matters in their own hands and to centralize power, ordered the nationalization of the railways, using foreign capital to carry out the plan. The provinces were furious and popular uprisings occurred in parts of the country. People refused to pay taxes, and strikes and demonstrations were organized. When the government ignored public demands, the railway issue merged with the revolutionary movement.

At the same time, Chinese banks had begun investing heavily in the phenomenal growth of the rubber trade in Malaya, but many of these investments proved worthless. Plantations that did not exist, were sold; rubber trees were planted and sold immediately although they would not yield for years. The bottom fell out of the rubber business. Railways were not built. There was a serious recession in trade and construction.

My father was worried by the trend of events. His company suffered losses and the future looked precarious. He began to consider moving to Canada, which he felt offered greater opportunities.

Ruth Ricketts was unhappy. An upheaval in her life work of dedication to the Chinese people was depressing, but the move seemed inevitable.

Father finally sailed for Vancouver early in 1911, to discover the possibilities of establishing himself there. Finding work with an electrical firm, he sent for Mother and me, and later in the spring of 1911, we left for Canada.

The parting was not easy. Our house boy, pleading to accompany us, was given permission to go to Canada, but my heart-broken amah sobbed her farewell as our boat set sail for a new land and a new life.

4. Years of Change

The year 1911 was one of the most important dates, both in my life and in modern Chinese history. For me, a mere toddler, it signalled the beginning of a new life in Canada. For China, it brought not only the end of the Manchu dynasty but the end of imperial rule for all time.

No massive civil war initiated the new era. One thing led to another with incompetence and treachery complicating events. The match that lit the fire was a railway fiasco in the province of Szechuan. The populace, angry because of government intervention in railway investments and the influx of foreign capital, protested loudly and actively. In early October of 1911, an imperial army was dispatched to quell the disturbance. But the government's weakened home base in Wuchang fell to local rebels. In rapid succession the revolts spread, and cities and provinces began seceding from the empire. Within six weeks, two-thirds of China had announced independence from royal rule. The Ch'ing rulers signed an abdication edict. Sun Yat-sen, in the United States at the time, rushed to Europe to seek the support of Britain and France, and then returned to Shanghai on December 25. Four days later he was elected provisional President of the Republic of China. January 1, 1912, was proclaimed the first day of the new republic.

My mother and father had high hopes for the new China. Like many foreigners, they saw Sun as a reasonable, educated Christian, dedicated to creating a revived and democratic nation. The end had finally come to 268 years of rule by the hated foreign Ch'ing dynasty of the Manchus and to more than two thousand years of imperial rule.

But Sun was a very unhappy man. Of his "Three Principles of the People" only the first — the overthrow of the Manchus and the development of a spirit of nationalism — was given any importance. The second and third principles, namely a democratic form of government and the improvement in the people's welfare, were all but forgotten.

Yuan Shi-kai, a wily, power-hungry general, had manoeuvred himself into the position of go-between with the Manchus and the revolutionaries. He had also secretly included in the Ch'ing abdication edict a clause authorizing him to organize a republican form of government.

Sun drew up a provisional constitution in February 1912, incorporating his three-stage revolutionary program. Faced, however, with Yuan's military strength and the lack of support for his three principles by even his own followers, he agreed to step down from the presidency in favour of the general.

Once in control, Yuan made a mockery of the revolution. Democratic rule became a farce. Through bribery and assassination, Yuan eliminated most opposition. When parliament finally met and rejected his demands, he surrounded the building with his troops and proclaimed his measures as law.

Sun, in spite of his thwarted plans, was still active and popular. Although much of his support came from overseas Chinese, his loyal collaborators at home attempted to reassert their power. When a second revolution in 1913 was crushed by Yuan, the populace, weary of the fighting, demanded a settlement of the differences. But Yuan's dream was to become a lifetime ruler — an emperor in all but name. By dissolving parliament and using threats, Yuan crushed all opposition, and by 1914, his dictatorship was assured. He also attained the right to nominate his own successor.

About this time, Yuan's education minister visited Canada. Some overseas Chinese had made their opposition to Yuan's government clear. The minister was murdered in Victoria. The murderer was never caught. The police ran up against a stone wall because the overseas Chinese, for the most part, supported Sun and nobody could — or would — give any evidence. The Christian pastor's home was raided by the Victoria police but nothing that would incriminate him or the church members was found. Pastors avoided political issues because they divided the congregation.

With the Western powers gripped by the First World War, Yuan extended his powers and came to terms with Japan. But when the Chinese people discovered that, in 1915, he had accepted Japan's "Twenty-one Demands," which practically placed China under Japanese control, their anger knew no bounds. Yuan didn't last long. Everyone who had trusted him now found him disloyal. His generals were jealous of each other and were always looking for personal power. His followers began to desert him. Japan, fearful of a strong China, did everything possible to weaken Yuan. Overtaken by a sudden illness, Yuan died on June 6, 1916.

The atmosphere of suspicion and lawlessness which had developed, led to years of warlords and near anarchy. Sun, in an attempt to revive his dream, organized a Constitution Protection campaign. He gathered round him all those who were disillusioned by both the imperial system and the years of so-called republicanism. Some students and intellectuals withdrew into academic life, but others began the search for a new solution. The revolution of 1911 had destroyed the old government but Chinese society had not yet been touched by change.

Mutinies, defections and betrayals dogged Sun's path. Civil war became the order of the day, and the government fell into the hands of whatever general happened to establish himself for the time being in the seat of government. The economy collapsed, floods and famine ravished the land, trade declined and what civil service there was disappeared. Generals were interested only in lining their own pockets, making fortunes in opium, prostitution and "squeeze" (the rakeoff at each level of a transaction). They sold official posts, taxed the populace beyond the limits of endurance and then retired to safe foreign colonies to live out their lives in ease.

In a desperate bid to restore order, Sun's supporters invited him to Peking in December of 1924, where he was warmly received by the people. But failing health diminished his powers, and on March 12, 1925, Sun died, a very frustrated and disappointed man. He had laid the foundations of democratic reform, however, and is now honoured as "the father of modern China."

Chaos continued and warlords ravished the country. Rural

landlords sucked the life blood of the peasants, leaving them weak and destitute, powerless to retaliate. Those unable to eke out an existence took to banditry.

"At this time," one woman told me many years later, "my mother and father both worked on a tea plantation. Even when they worked fourteen to sixteen hours a day, seven days a week, they could not make enough to keep our family of five. They would go out on the hillside at night and cut brushwood to peddle in town to make a few extra cents. As soon as I was able I was in the fields too, from dawn till dark. I was the oldest of three daughters."

"Were you reasonably well treated?" I asked.

She scoffed at the idea. "If we did not pick fast enough to suit the overseer, he would lay a whip across our backs. I saw welts rise and sometimes the blood run down my father's back. If my father was too weak to move quickly the overseer would turn wild dogs on him.

"Life was short and we often longed to die. When I was thirteen years old, my father took ill. There was no treatment or medicine for him, and within six months he was dead. My mother was expecting a child, and there was no way she could support us all, so she gave my ten-year-old sister to a friend who volunteered to keep her. My four-year-old sister went into the landlords's house, but within two years she was blind from malnutrition and abuse and came home to die. When the baby was born, it was another girl, so my mother threw her away in the garbage."

I gasped. Then I recalled the large bins outside the village walls where girl babies were frequently thrown at birth. It seemed so callous, and yet, was it not kinder than the alternatives of starvation, slavery or prostitution? Moreover, girls became the property of their husband's family at marriage and were often treated as slaves. A girl was just another mouth to feed, offering no security to her parents in their old age.

As the woman spoke, I thought of my own childhood and teen years, full of fun and activities: school, sports, music and family holidays.

We had stayed in Vancouver for two years before Father had accepted a position in Moose Jaw, Saskatchewan. Here the Chinese community was small and not highly organized, but Mother, as usual, sought out the Chinese residents and became acquainted.

One of my first clear childhood recollections was dated August 4, 1914. I distinctly recall the five-inch black headlines in the newspaper —

WAR. Although I was not quite five, I sensed my parents' concern and knew something serious had happened.

After the birth of my sister in July, 1915, we moved to Quebec City where Father was engaged in war work, but the following year found us in Toronto. Only eight months elapsed before Father, in 1916, was transferred to Winnipeg by his firm, the Canadian General Electric Company. My mother, brought up in an English Methodist manse, was heard to remark, "At least as a minister's daughter I was sure of three years in one place!"

Winnipeg was home from 1916 to 1926, and the arrival of my brother increased our family number to five. In Winnipeg, Mother and Father found a large Chinese community and worked unreservedly with its members. I counted many Chinese people as friends, and the Chinese language was a familiar sound in our home. The Chinese minister's family were frequent visitors in our house, and years later, his daughters and I reminisced about sharing a crib when the family came over for the evening.

Active work amongst the Chinese was undertaken by the churches of Canada, particularly in providing educational opportunities and recreation. Young Methodist Church, one of the largest in Winnipeg, had a separate Chinese department in the Sunday School attended by many immigrant men wishing to learn more English.

One of my pleasant Sunday duties as a little girl was to help a young Chinese man who came regularly to our house for half an hour before the Sunday afternoon class. I was detailed to help him learn and pronounce the words of the hymns that would be sung. I never succeeded in changing his "Jesus shwabes" to "Jesus saves", but at least we both enjoyed the reading sessions. Athletic clubs were also encouraged and my father worked actively with a group of Chinese men in a "Y" gym class. Eventually the non-Christian Chinese set up their much-loved secret societies with athletic committees, encouraging the martial arts known as wushu or kungfu, and out of these developed the physically demanding folk and dragon dances.

But the aim of every Chinese immigrant was education for their children. An old Chinese friend of mine — Moore Whaun he called himself — told me, much later, of his struggles in the early years of the century.

"My parents owned a shop in South China and managed to save enough to help me with my passage," he explained. "I came to Canada by myself in 1907, at the age of fourteen. I still had a pigtail. 'Queues,' as they were called, were decreed by the Manchus as a sign of subservience. Anyone disobeying the law was decapitated. I didn't cut off my pigtail when I came here because I didn't want to be ostracized by the Chinese community.

"It was very difficult getting into Canada — a really frustrating experience. I spent more than a week in the immigration sheds in Victoria, but eventually I was allowed to land."

"How did you manage to support yourself and get an education when you were so young, without the language, and entirely on your own?" I asked in amazement.

"I worked at any job I could get. I washed dishes, helped in a corner store and in a mill, worked on a farm — anything to survive. Then I was fortunate to be taken in by a Canadian family for a time. They gave me food and a place to sleep in return for work around their home. There was no pay but it gave me the chance to learn the language. I was determined to get an education. I graduated from high school and eventually from the University of British Columbia in 1927. It wasn't easy."

This I knew, for in the last two years of his university life, he was a fellow student with my husband. Moore Whaun's wife, a pastor's daughter, graduated with me two years later.

"There was so much discrimination against Orientals and talk of the 'yellow peril'," he recalled. "In 1906, rioters attacked Chinatown, and in the end, the government had to award the Chinese residents $100,000 indemnity for damages. We were denied privileges in public places, in shops and clubs, and the professions were not open to us. But I firmly believed that a sense of self-importance was the key. If you lost your self-respect you were in trouble."

When I asked him how he managed to get a job, he rose and paced the floor. "I was just lucky," he said. "Before I graduated, I was offered work with one of the big Chinese daily newspapers published in Vancouver, and I've been in newspaper work every since. At ninety, I'm still writing, and I only retired from my newspaper job nine years ago."

He pulled files from his cupboards and desk and showed me letters from all over the world. Presidents and prime ministers, professors, writers and scientists and many other men and women corresponded with him over the years. The determined shopkeeper's son had not only seen, but participated in, nearly a century of change and upheaval.

"You know," he added, "you had to be a saint to stay decent in those early days. Illegal opium and gambling dens or houses of ill-repute were the only places where the men were welcome. It was a hard and lonely life. But I must say there were devoted Canadians, particularly the church womenfolk, who gave hours of their time to teach us English and organize activities."

I remembered how my mother and father spent days and nights responding to the needs of the Chinese community. On occasions my mother, because of her fluency in the language, was called to interpret for immigration or hospital authorities. But her chief delight was visiting in the homes where Chinese women were often isolated by language barriers. She would also drop in to the many Chinese laundries which existed in the teens and twenties. With amusement she recounted one such visit.

One day she went into a laundry and spoke in Chinese to the old gentleman at the desk.

"No speakee English," he said.

"Ngoh kong tong wa," said Mother, indicating that she could speak Chinese.

The old man shook his head, waved his hands, and repeated, "No speakee English."

In slow, clear tones Mother then said in English, "I speak Chinese."

His face lit up. "Speakee Chinese," he said in disbelief, and then the conversation flowed rapidly. "You come some more," he said when the dialogue concluded, and thereafter Mother was a welcome visitor.

Not only did Mother call on homes and businesses, but every vegetable pedlar seemed to call on us. At Christmas, Oriental generosity showered us with everything from boxed dried lichee, turkeys and chocolates to silks and ornaments. On one occasion, a sack which had been deposited in our hallway suddenly moved, and we discovered the present was a live duck.

Many of the men who settled in Canada at the turn of the century, were workmen brought from China to help in the building of the Canadian Pacific Railway. Others participated in the gold rush. Lacking capital or much knowledge of the English language, they established themselves as cooks and laundrymen. Life was hard, and where there were little children, they too shared the long hours of work. Rising early, the youngsters would stoke the fires and carry bundles of laundry before they set off for school. Education was precious to these people. "Every coolie's son a scholar" was their motto.

But a number of the laundrymen had no small boys to help and no mother to care for the home. The majority of the Chinese who came to Canada through the first decades of this century were single men. The entry of Chinese women and families was discouraged by the Canadian government. A head tax of fifty dollars was required for each Chinese immigrant, and in 1901, this was raised to one hundred dollars. In 1904, the tax was raised again to five hundred dollars. This prohibitive restriction was an insidious piece of discrimination, as it applied only to the Chinese people. In spite of the levy, families pooled their resources and chose certain male members to go in search of a living in Canada, and they in turn sent back money to China to help sustain their poverty stricken families. The head tax netted the Canadian government an average of one million dollars a year in revenue.

As the Chinese community in Winnipeg grew, an interdenominational Chinese church was established with living quarters for single men. Regular classes were organized for English-language study. Times of services and lessons had to be adapted to the long hours of work and the minimal free time of the laundry and restaurant workers.

Politics, because of its divisiveness, was for the most part banished, so it was impossible to get information from the Chinese themselves about events in China. Much of our information came from missionaries returning on leave, some of whom had hair-raising stories to tell of experiences encountered as a result of continuous civil strife.

The second decade of the century was chaotic in China. The West, far too busy with World War One, was unconcerned about developments in Asia. Chinese industry however, expanded as a result of the war, and a larger merchant and labour force began to join the intellectuals in demanding self-determination. A powerful intellectual revolution was producing a new literature based on the vernacular instead of the classical language, and this dealt a shattering blow to many old traditions. A new freedom of expression and thought was beginning to emerge from the universities, and books and magazines poured out new and exciting ideas.

In 1917, China entered the war on the side of the allies, and Chinese workers went to Europe to work on roads and in dockyards and factories. Returning to their homeland, they brought back new ideas. More important still, the Russian Revolution of 1917 had a profound effect on China. Marxism had first made its appearance in China in 1905, with the translation of Marx's biography and some of Engel's works. Lenin's fight against imperialism struck a sympathetic note in China. China was ripe for change.

5. Unrest and Protest

November 11, 1918, was an exciting day in Winnipeg. I can remember walking down Portage Avenue with my father as the crowds shouted, whistles blared and anything that made a noise was used. The war was over, and the sense of relief was overwhelming. I was only nine years old, but I too, was caught up in the excitement and celebration.

In China, there had been celebrations as well. The Chinese rejoiced in the victory of democracy — or so they thought. The Chinese delegation went off to the Peace Conference in Versailles with great hope. China, they believed, would now be treated with justice. All the injustices of the past — extraterritoriality, foreign control of customs and courts and indemnity payments — would be wiped out. Unfortunately it didn't happen that way.

Those who had celebrated the war's end and had waited with eagerness for the peace settlement found that the warlord regime in Peking had made secret treaties with Japan. The treaties gave Japan the right to take over Germany's sphere of influence in Shantung province. Japan was also permitted to build railways, station Japanese troops there and control and train the insidious railway guards.

China's representatives in Versailles were furious. President Wilson of the United States objected to the treatment of China because he believed in national self-determination and wanted to abolish secret diplomacy. He became a hero to the Chinese. But his objections were overruled. The other nations didn't wish to oppose Japan. When Japan refused to join the League of Nations unless the treaty was honoured, Wilson weakened.

Students in Peking sent thousands of telegrams to the Chinese delegation in Paris. Chinese students studying in Paris organized a twenty-four hour watch on the hotel where the Chinese delegation was staying, and prevented them from leaving to sign the Treaty of Versailles.

Meanwhile in China, a momentous event took place. The May Fourth Demonstration was called by some, the first genuine mass movement in modern Chinese history. The Chinese people were violently angry with the Western powers. They felt betrayed. Five thousand people joined the students in Peking in a mass protest.

I remembered missionaries, returned from China, describing how the protest spread. Merchants and consumers boycotted Japanese goods; dockhands refused to unload Japanese freight.

"My father and my uncle marched in that May Fourth Demonstration," a Chinese friend told me. "It was the turning point in their lives. My uncle was so frustrated, he buried himself in the study of Chinese philosophy and history, at the same time trying to work out a programme of democratic social reform. But my father turned to Marxist socialism. He joined a Marxist study group and continued his studies at Peking University which became a centre of radical thought."

At this point, Mao Tse-tung became involved. Dr. Li, the librarian at Peking University, founded the New Tide Society. Li's library assistant was Mao Tse-tung. When Dr. Li was soon executed by one of the warlords, Mao took his place. Dr. Li had persuaded Mao that the peasants were the key to revolution in China.

In July, 1921, Mao helped to found the Communist Party, but the Party soon split. The Shanghai section favoured the Russian plan to base the revolution on the industrial workers in the cities, but the Peking group, led by Mao, believed that guerilla tactics using the peasants was the way to go.

Sun Yat-sen was still alive at that time and the Russians suggested that the Communists join his party, called the Kuomintang. They all seemed to be working for the same ideals, the Russians argued.

Reluctantly Sun agreed to this arrangement, although he was concerned the new recruits might prove too powerful.

Meanwhile Chiang Kai-shek, a promising young officer, had been sent by Dr. Sun to Moscow for military training. When he returned he opened the Whampoa Military Academy near Canton and set out to build up a modern army. In the light of Chiang's future actions it was an ironic situation.

China was very remote. News in the early twenties was not yet instantaneous. Father brought home an early radio set and we pricked the crystal, searching for the spot that would bring in the sound. But the daily papers were still the chief source of news. First-hand knowledge came often from returning missionaries and the word was "confusion." Hopes were pinned on Sun Yat-sen. The West waited, although for the most part, somewhat indifferently.

Torn between the need for Communist ties with labour and the peasants and the fear of the growing Communist movement, Sun, in the closing years of his life, agreed to the principle of cooperation. The Russians sent their advisers and a joint manifesto was issued in 1923. The following January, the First National Congress of the United Front was held, but the congress was disrupted when news arrived of Lenin's death. With the death of Dr. Sun the following year, the alliance fell apart.

At this time, in the late fall of 1925, my father decided to move the family back to Vancouver. He went on ahead to get established and my mother, brother and sister joined him early in 1926. I remained in Winnipeg to complete my first year at Manitoba University. I then transferred to the University of British Columbia. Closer proximity to the Orient and the large Chinese community in Vancouver brought the Chinese situation closer to us. Among the Chinese, there was a great deal of ill-feeling between the anti-revolutionists and the reform league.

"One night when I was working over-time in our office on Pender Street in Vancouver's Chinatown," Moore Whaun, my journalist friend had told me. "I came back from supper to find the police at the newspaper office door. I was told I could not go inside. While I was at supper, someone had gone into the office and murdered one of our newspaper men. We were almost certain who was responsible but it was never proved in court. Indications were that it was a member of the opposing party who ran the rival newspaper." Once again Chinese politics had reached deep into Canada.

Those of us who followed events in China looked on with concern. Who would pick up the pieces now that Sun Yat-sen was gone?

Chiang Kai-shek had set up the military academy in Canton, and with his officers and cadets, he had put down uprisings in the South. He was then appointed by the Kuomintang Government as Commander-in-Chief of their army. We now looked on Chiang as the saviour of China. He appeared to be restoring some semblance of order, and his march against the warlords seemed a good idea. Everyone longed for peace and unification.

The Soviet Union sent supplies, while their Communist agents organized peasants and workers. Chiang meanwhile took city after city. By March 1927, his forces had entered Nanking and were marching on Shanghai. It had taken him only nine months to conquer the southern half of China.

But the Communist and nationalist unions just wouldn't work together. The Communists did not trust the right wing of the Nationalist party. The Nationalists resented the fact that the Communists still remained members of their own party, although they were also in the Kuomintang.

"It was bitter medicine," said a young Communist to me. "We controlled Shanghai through a strong labour union. Moscow asked us to co-operate with Chiang, so when he came into the city we supported him. The Traitor!"

I urged him to explain. "Once inside the city," he said, "Chiang lined up with the financiers and big businesses who formed a 'Purge Committee' to liquidate the Communists. The Communist headquarters were raided, men were shot and the unions were destroyed."

Western news did not convey these facts. Britain, however, along with the United States, France, Italy, Japan, Belgium, the Netherlands, Portugal and China, endorsed a Nine-Power Treaty as a sign of goodwill. But there was no way to enforce the agreement, which actually did little to eliminate the privileges that powers had in China. Foreigners still treated the Chinese with arrogance, and they held controlling posts in the Customs, Postal Service and Salt Tax Levies. Extraterritoriality — the control of areas within Chinese cities by foreign governments — meant that Chinese paid taxes to foreign governments without any representation on municipal councils. The Japanese were encroaching still further into Manchuria. Students and the growing labour class were restless. Violent clashes occurred.

"I was in China doing some study and research," a Canadian friend told me, "when I was trapped by some of the uprisings. I saw the French and British gunning down students because of anti-foreign demonstrations."

When I was in Shanghai in 1976, our guide pointed to a street. "That," he said, "is the scene of the May 30 massacre of 1926. It was a black day in our history."

A strike to protest low wages in a Japanese mill in Shanghai had led to violence. Some Chinese workers were killed. At a memorial service for the dead some of the students and workers were arrested. This incited a demonstration by 3,000 students on Nanking Road, protesting British and Japanese action. Nervous British forces fired on the demonstrators, and this act touched off nation-wide violence. Strikes, protests and boycotts followed.

As students in Canada, some of us were deeply concerned. We protested British "gun-boat diplomacy." At a hot meeting at the University of British Columbia, we spoke out against extraterritoriality, foreign control of Chinese courts, taxation without representation in the Shanghai International Settlement and the constant dictation of policies to China by foreign powers. Ashamed when British gun-boats were sent up the rivers of China, we students argued with people who insisted that the Western powers had to protect their citizens and their national privileges.

"Do you blame them for revolting," we said, "when foreigners put up signs saying *No Dogs Or Chinese Allowed Here* — right in their own city?"

Many of my friends at University were Chinese, Japanese and East Indian. Although they were chiefly second-generation Canadians — as there were very few exchange students at that time — they were very conscious of the indignities suffered by their countrymen.

An intense wave of pacifism was sweeping the West. We applauded the Kellogg-Briand Pact of 1928, which outlawed war as a means of settling international disputes. A packed auditorium at a noon-hour meeting at the University of British Columbia, demanded dissolution of the Officers Training Corp programme at the university. In those days

Ghandi was a hero, and his passive resistance movement in India stirred our sympathies.

But public student demonstrations in Europe and America were not the order of the day. Students in the West had never been imbued with the same sense of mission which characterized their counterparts in China. Scholars in China were at the top of the social ladder and were regarded with honour and respect.

In imperial days, students worked towards the incredible examinations which were the only entrance to the world of officialdom. Confucianism had embedded in Chinese society a sense of responsibility, for those who possessed knowledge, to become the models and saviours of their country.

With the abolition of these examinations in republican China, students still maintained that sense of privilege and position. As the proud possessors of an education, they instinctively considered themselves destined to be agents of change. They continually played a major part in national affairs and assumed leadership roles.

"My father nearly paid with his life for his student activist beliefs," one young woman in China told me. "He managed to escape from the Shanghai massacre and went to join the left wing of the Nationalist Party who were still allied with the Communists. But a Communist-sponsored uprising in July 1927, led to the reunion of the left and right wings of the Nationalists, and the Communists were wiped out. My father was left for dead, but some workers found him and saved his life. He escaped and went to join Mao Tse-tung who was organizing the peasants in Hunan province. He stayed with Mao for many years, helping him to harass the Nationalists. My mother and I did not see him again for many years."

Meanwhile, with the help of German officers, Chiang built up a trained army of half a million men. He made strange alliances with some of the warlords, managing to trade off regional power for some kind of support. But the whole situation was very unstable. He was never able to stop the growth of the Communist forces in spite of waging constant war against them. Revolts were continually breaking out which cost the nation huge sums of money. To add to the confusion, Japan did not want a strong China. She began to interfere in the north and to do everything possible to destabilize the incompetent Chinese regime.

6. Return to China

While China was struggling with civil war, Japanese encroachment and party strife, I was struggling in Vancouver with university examinations, practise teaching and job applications. In May of 1929, I completed my B.A., returning in September to enter my professional year for my teacher's certificate.

At student discussion groups we had often talked of the present economic system, and my Father and I had attended discussions in the League for Social Reconstruction. Two friends and I had written a letter to the editor of a national magazine pointing out some of our concerns. The letter had been centrally boxed and then damned with faint praise. But like most people we were unprepared for the Wall Street Crash and were totally unaware of its implications. Only time eventually revealed its enormous impact.

In the spring of 1930, with my teacher's certificate in hand, I began applying for a teaching position, but it was a waste of paper and stamps. Only a dozen or so of the 125 university education graduates found schools, and those chiefly through special contacts in their small home towns. My fiance, Dick Phillips, had also taken his teacher training at the University of British Columbia. Together we applied for positions, then waited and waited for an appointment which never came. For the next two years, only the rare substitute teaching job occurred.

Then, in the summer of 1932, an incidental meeting changed our lives. Returning from a walk one evening Dick and I were greeted at the door by my Mother.

"Mrs. Lewis has just called," she said. "Her husband was talking by chance to a school principal from Canton who is holidaying in Vancouver. She remarked that, if she could find a suitable woman teacher, she would be prepared to take her on staff at her school."

Dick and I looked at one another in dismay. A job was a job, but we hardly anticipated a separation of eight thousand miles.

The next day, however, I was on the principal's doorstep timidly broaching the subject. I wasn't sure what I wanted. I was torn between the exciting prospect and the wrench of leaving. The principal explained that all instruction at the school was given in English in the senior grades, since the girls wrote the matriculation exams for Hong Kong University which was associated with Cambridge University. This meant I would not require language study but would begin teaching as soon as I arrived.

We talked for some time and then she said, "I'm prepared to take you if you will come for a three-year term." Three years was a long time at this period of my life. Sensing my indecision she added, "I'm leaving for Banff tomorrow morning. Why not think it over and wire me at the hotel. I'm returning to China in a week, but you could follow in three weeks."

I must have been a driving hazard as I made my way home. China had never been in my thoughts for the future, yet it all seemed to fall into place. I had the background. I would be living close to my birthplace; there were still people in Canton who would remember my parents.

"I'll get a school one of these days," Dick said, "and we'll be married when you come home."

So, in September 1932, I sailed for Hong Kong, a trip of two-and-a-half weeks across the Pacific and down the China coast. My family and fiance were, of course, at the dock to see me off. Once the ship was under way, they raced in our old Essex car to the First Narrows lookout for a final farewell as the great white *Hikawa Maru* steamed through the narrow pass leading to the Straits of Juan de Fuca and the open sea. Too excited to shed tears, I set forth on an adventure which changed the course of my life.

My cabin mate was an older American woman returning from a visit to the States to rejoin her husband, a businessman in Japan. Her accounts of life in Japan were entertaining, and our Japanese cabin boy added his own story. He and his family had experienced the terrible Japanese earthquake of 1925. From the news stories we had read and from his description we sensed some of the trauma his family had experience in the Tokyo holocaust.

Life on board was leisurely and interesting. After a few days of practice, tennis and shuffleboard competitions were organized, and they both added some excitement to the day. Two days out from Japan, we met the fishboats. I was alarmed at what seemed to me to be the danger they faced in the heavy seas, but no one else appeared to regard the situation as hazardous. We ploughed on, leaving the little boats bobbing up and down on the peaks and troughs of the high waves.

When the ship docked in Yokohama, my cabin mate left to join her husband. I, along with some of the other passengers, disembarked and took the train the short distance to Tokyo, where we spent a few hours shopping and sightseeing. Then it was back on board again and on to Kobe where we watched the labourers, mostly women, carrying baskets of coal up the gangplanks to refuel the ship.

Once on the high seas again, we set sail for Shanghai. My Mother's friend in Vancouver had written to a friend in Shanghai, asking her to meet me and take me around the city for the single day the ship was docked there. For one who had never lived away from a comfortable but simple home (except for two months on summer jobs while at university), it was a strange experience.

I was whisked away in a chauffeur-driven limousine around the huge, unfamiliar city, shown the race track — which I gathered was an important social rendezvous for the foreign community — and then taken to a vast antique and arts and craft store. There I saw floors of Chinese porcelain, cloisonne, carved furniture, scrolls, paintings, carvings, lacquer ware; a breath-taking array. Unfortunately there was only time for a cursory glimpse of these oriental treasures. Luncheon was served at my hostess's mansion (as it seemed to me), where we were waited on by well-trained, courteous servants; a lifestyle totally unfamiliar to me.

I was almost glad to be back on the ship again in the late afternoon. Alone in my now familiar cabin, I wondered what I would find at my final port of call, Hong Kong.

The weather was getting hotter and more humid, and I found my

Canadian summer clothes not very suitable for the heat. As the depression years had made new clothes a luxury, my wardrobe was sparse. No one had warned me that rayon was unsuitable for the tropics and silk stockings here hot. But despite some discomfort, life aboard was exciting. The games and entertainment were fun and the constant passing of junks and small fishboats or coastal steamers added interest.

Daily now, tropical fruits were appearing on the menu. The morning after we left Shanghai, a pomelo arrived on my table. As I eyed this large pear-shaped fruit, I wondered if I was supposed to eat it all. Fortunately, my more knowledgeable table companions arrived and explained that one only removed as many pieces of the fruit as one wanted. Each segment had been separated and replaced in the lower half of the thick skin which served as a fruit bowl. Immediately acquiring a liking for this sweet grapefruit-like fruit I looked forward to encountering it again. Assuredly, next morning there it sat but surrounded by little squat bananas, a variety of oranges, and what I thought were tomatoes. But the "tomatoes" turned out to be bright red persimmons and I was introduced to yet another delicious new taste experience.

By the third day, my excitement was mounting. I approached the colony of Hong Kong with eager curiosity. This was my birthplace, my home for the first two and a half years of my life. A four-foot-long panoramic picture of the island and harbour had always hung in our home. As we came through Lymoon Pass, the narrow strait between the mainland and the north end of Hong Kong Island, I saw "the Peak," the formation which made the island of Hong Kong so distinct. Only a waterfront road and two streets ran level along the coast. After that, the road began to wind steeply up the mountainside. For those wealthy residents who could afford to live at the top, the cable tram was the common form of transport.

Our liner moved through the beautiful harbour. I was fascinated by it all: the hundreds of sampans and junks, the busy little Star Ferry still running back and forth every ten minutes from island to mainland, the British navy ships anchored in line down the centre of the harbour and, in a parallel line, steamers and cargo ships from all over the world.

I scanned the upturned faces of the crowd waiting on the dock below. Somewhere there must be a friendly figure come to greet me. Moving from the deck rail to the reception area near the purser's office, I soon heard an English voice say, "Are you by any chance Molly Ricketts?" Miss Upsdell, one of the teachers from the school in Canton, introduced herself and, under her direction, my trunk and bag were dispatched to the night boat for Canton.

"We have several hours before we leave," she said. "First I'm going to take you to St. Stephen's Girls School and introduce you to our Hong Kong Mission staff."

From the pier we walked a short distance along the waterfront to the Star Ferry and crossed to the island. Rickshaw coolies besieged us as soon as we landed, but the school was on an upper level road and we caught a bus. Roads ran parallel along the side of the Peak, joined at intervals by "S" turns so cars and buses could wind their way up the mountainside.

I was warmly greeted by the English staff when we arrived in time for lunch. Both St. Stephen's Girls and Boys Schools in Hong Kong and St. Hilda's — to which I was going in Canton — were run by the English Anglican Church. Close to the girls' school was an excellent mission hospital. On the same level was an Anglican-run student hostel connected with the University of Hong Kong.

During the afternoon, we rode on the tram up the vertical side of the Peak, passing houses and apartments, precariously but nevertheless solidly, perched on the mountainside. My father had often described that famous tram ride. He had been, in his day, responsible for some of the electrical work on the cable car. In the somewhat cooler air at the very top were the homes of the well-to-do and some small elite hospitals.

The panoramic view from the top was fascinating.The long, enclosed harbour stretched from the pass in the north to the many small islands enclosing its southern entrance. What appeared as minute figures and miniature cars and buses moved along the waterfront, while the harbour provided an endless procession of boats. Across the harbour, Kowloon and other settlements stretched to the far hills which separated the leased New Territories from China proper.

On the far side of the Peak lay fishing villages, and at the northern tip, not visible from the Peak, was the prestigious St. Stephen's Boys School. A million people lived in this compact area — some in squalor, many in borderline poverty, others in relative comfort, and a few in lavish surroundings — presided over by a governor appointed by the British Crown, and an appointed council.

Beyond the distant hills lay China, and I was anxious to reach the end of my journey. Canton was only a three-hour train ride from Kowloon, but because the night trip by steamer was a pleasant method of travel, particularly with baggage, we left at 10:00 p.m. My Father had taken this same journey in 1904. Here I was, embarking on the identical trip in 1932, to begin, like him, a new life in a strange land. What would it hold for me? Would it influence my life as it had my parents'?

At six o'clock the next morning, our boat eased its way through the mass of junks and sampans to the dock already seething with people. But while the ship was still several feet from her berth, shouting coolies leapt the distance to the railings and, vying for patronage, surrounded the passengers, particularly the affluent foreigners. Two dozen hands seized my bags as my companion bargained for the services of one man. When he was finally selected, the other disappointed coolies rushed off elsewhere. A tip meant the difference between food and an empty belly.

When the din and confusion had subsided somewhat, we disembarked, and once more the haggling began, this time for a car for ourselves and another for my bag and trunk. The bargaining over, the driver's lackey went off to collect the luggage and we drove away in our car.

"Do we just leave the bags?" I gasped as I thought of my possessions sitting on the wharf.

"They'll be along shortly," said Miss Upsdell cheerfully, and true enough they arrived at the school within the hour.

I was astonished at the noise and the hazards of the road. Along the side of the street ran the rickshaw coolies. Their hair-raising screams — at pedestrians who interrupted their stride — were reminiscent of the dying shrieks of a werewolf. Crowds walked on the roads because the sidewalks were pre-empted by street vendors, beggars, children at play and the furniture of those who had moved out of their hot tenements to sleep and eat on the pavements. Miraculously, the crowd parted as a car or bus approached and then merged again. The vehicle was constantly engulfed.

"Why does the driver continuously blow his horn?" I asked, as our chauffeur blasted his way down the street.

"Buses and cars are required to have two horns to get the attention of pedestrians," explained Miss Upsdell. Judging by the universal disregard for the warning signs I questioned the validity of the regulation. "You'll get used to it and pay no more attention than any one else," concluded

Miss Upsdell cheerfully. As she spoke, the battery-powered "beep-beep" and the throaty "whoof" of the hand-operated bulb horn both went into operation again. The driver handled the car with one hand on the wheel and the other constantly on one or other of the horns.

The car came to an abrupt stop as a flock of ducks, led by a small boy, crossed the road. Starting up, the car narrowly missed a line of blind beggars, whose sightless leader prodded the road with his stick and whined for alms. Bicycles swerved in and out of the crowd, avoiding people, rickshaws, water buffaloes, hand-drawn carts and buses.

After four miles of this amazing disorder, we arrived at the door of the school and rang the gong for the doorkeeper. A kindly woman answered our summons and I was welcomed into St. Hilda's School, my home for the next two and a half years.

7. Life at St. Hilda's

As the heavy doors swung shut and the doorkeeper dropped the bars, I looked around. I was standing on a stone floor in a small entrance with dark wood archways and grey brick corridors stretching on either side across the front of the school. The windowless wall on the street side kept out the sights and some of the noise of the road. The corridors led on one side to the dormitories and on the other to the classrooms.

"We'll have some breakfast and then I'll show you around the premises," said Miss Upsdell. "But come up to your room first and have a wash."

We walked from the entrance to a large grey stone hallway, and then to the three-storey box which was the accommodation for the foreign staff. It was a square building squeezed between the corridor to the dormitories and a small patio without any consideration for the aesthetics of the original premises. On the ground floor were the amahs' rooms and the bathroom, a euphonious term for the chemical toilets and native clay tubs into which we dumped our daily bucket of bath water. The second and third floors consisted of three square rooms on each floor, one of which was a small sitting room. In my room, what looked like a four-poster turned out to be a bed complete with a mosquito net which hung from a height of eight feet, and was tucked in under the mattress at night to provide protection from the malarial mosquitoes.

The rooms were very plain, but windows back and front permitted a through breeze when there happened to be one. I was soon to discover that they also permitted the entrance of hordes of mosquitoes. In the end I had my windows screened, although my colleagues warned me that I would suffocate. I chose suffocation and survived, never regretting my decision.

Having seen my bags deposited in my room on that first morning, I started off on the tour of inspection.

"I should explain," said Miss Upsdell, "that this school was originally a Buddhist Temple and a City of the Dead."

"Sounds fascinating," I murmured, although the chatter of girls and the clatter of wooden "k'eks" (clogs) on the cement floors shattered the image.

When the Anglicans first bought the property, it had extended considerably further in front, but the city decided to put through a wide road and the school was notified to cut back. If the wall was moved by a certain date — the school was informed — the bricks from the wall could be kept. No compensation was offered. The result was that the tennis court was destroyed and hallways made narrower.

The classrooms were a number of small rooms with three walls, the fourth side entirely open to a garden courtyard. This was very pleasant during most of the year, but in the six or eight weeks of cold, clammy weather, it was decidedly uncomfortable, and some of the girls suffered chilblains from the cold stone floors. The classrooms had originally been the chambers where the bodies, hermetically sealed in coffins, were laid awaiting the auspicious day of burial. For the wealthy, that burial date was often a considerable time in coming, since the priests received offerings each day from the family.

At the end of the stone corridor, we came to a small two-storey wooden building which had been added for extra classrooms. "This is where your classes will be," said Miss Upsdell. "But when the wind is from the south-east, keep your windows shut. A rubber shoe factory has been built next door. They used our wall and just attached their building to it. The smell of hot rubber is rather overpowering."

At that moment a deafening roar startled me. "Only a plane taking off," explained my companion. "They've built a runway down the street and the planes just miss our chimney pots." Certainly this school did not resemble anything I had known. I was to discover more hazards as time went on.

As we walked through the school, curious eyes and whispers followed me. When we reached the senior classes on the second floor of the wooden building, I was introduced to the girls I was to teach. A warm welcome awaited me, and as time went on, lifelong friendships were forged.

Returning from our tour of inspection for "elevenses," which meant the tea break, we entered the staff reception and tea room. I gazed around in amazement. The dark wooden walls were fully sixteen feet high, the top three feet intricately carved in open latticework. At one end stood a massive stone altar; at the other end stood a delicately carved devil screen. Chinese devils move in a straight line. A devil screen placed inside a doorway prevented the conniving devil from making an entrance. Humans, however, could pass around the obstacle to right or left.

The reception room opened on to a wide verandah which ran completely around a garden patio. Meals were served on the verandah most of the year. During the few cold weeks, we ate in the Abbot's bedroom, a shadowy, windowless room with one hanging bulb installed for our convenience. The kitchen took up one side of the patio and, from behind its walls, stretched a long rope to a punkah above the dining table. The kitchen boy kept the punkah — a long woven bamboo shade — flapping back and forth during mealtime to cool the air.

On the far side of the patio was a charming moon-gate, the beautiful round doorway so typical of Chinese architecture. It was the entrance into the women's school. We had on staff the English principal of the women's school, who supervised the training of bible women and deaconesses. About fifty girls were in residence in St. Hilda's Girls School, approximately a third of the students. Their dormitories and dining hall were on the far side of the premises.

Before I completed my inspection, the gong sounded. We were recalled to the verandah meal table to join the headmistress who had engaged me in Vancouver, the Women's School principal and two other mission staff members. Some brought mosquito coils which burned under the table, and fans were on hand to add to the slight breeze from the punkah overhead.

After lunch there was a brief time for rest, and then I was invited to visit "next door." Passing through the dormitory section of the school, we came to a large doorway. A knock brought an amah to unlock the door and we were met by Gertrude Wittenbach. She was the daughter of the former mission secretary, and had met her Australian husband when he had arrived as pastor for the Canton mission. They had a pleasant home as part of the mission compound and a new baby enlivened life for us all.

During the course of a sumptuous tea with the Wittenbachs, Gertrude casually remarked, "The inmates were noisy last night. I wonder what the trouble was." When she saw my quizzical glance she explained that we were next to an insane asylum and, particularly at night, one could often hear the clanking of chains or the curses of the inmates. I wondered what next to expect.

After tea, I finished unpacking my things. As I did so, staff members would pop in and remark: "Here's some powder. Dust all your books with it or the silverfish will eat them." Or they would cheerfully warn: "Check your drawer regularly to make sure the white ants aren't chewing through the wood."

With these reassuring comments, I managed to set out my few belongings. After dinner at seven, I was ready to climb into my little mosquito-net house and, in spite of the heat, fall asleep. At six the next morning, I was aroused by the deep clanging of the school gong which happened to hang under my window. The street outside was already bustling with life. Food vendors pushed their carts while loudly touting their wares. Horns were beginning to blare, and rickshaw coolies were starting their long and wearying day. Added to the usual din was the rhythmic thumping of several hundred feet, as the army jogged past my window chanting in tonic "soh-fa." I discovered that the army barracks and parade grounds were immediately behind our school. Inside the walls, the kitchen staff were noisily banging pans and buckets, and the clop-clop of the wooden k'eks indicated that the resident girls and amahs were up and about.

Soon the day pupils would be arriving. When St. Hilda's School first opened after World War One, the non-resident students arrived primly in covered sedan chairs or escorted by their servant women who carried their books and parasols. Boarders never left the school unless a member of the family called for them.

What a different picture presented itself now. I was to see students jumping off the bus, sometimes without even waiting for it to stop, or arguing with the rickshaw coolies over fares.

School began at 8:30 with morning prayers, when all the girls in their grey and white pin-striped Chinese dresses filed into the chapel. I was pressed into service as organist. Frequently, a preying mantis would perch on the lamp shelf of the old organ with his legs in prayerful attitude all through the service. He became a little friend I looked for every day.

After chapel, the classes — taught by the three foreign teachers and a staff of English-speaking Chinese women — began, and carried on until 12:45. Following tiffin, the Chinese masters moved in. Sitting on their little platforms behind their desks, they dispensed traditional Chinese education to those students sufficiently interested to pay serious attention. The monotonous droning and recitation sometimes taxed the children's powers of concentration, particularly the younger ones.

School was in session on Saturday mornings with Wednesday and Saturday afternoons free. On their afternoon off, these modern boarders waited anxiously to sign out. Most of the girls managed to produce valid excuses for going out on half holidays. On Sundays, the boarders all attended the Chinese Anglican Church in the city, and Miss Upsdell and I took turns shepherding them to the service, a welcome half-hour walk from the school.

I found the girls very friendly and responsive, particularly the senior students with whom I was more closely associated. We were able to establish a happy relationship and I was touched when the Grade Ten class said one day, "Please close your eyes. Now open them. We give our hearts to you." There they all stood with little heart-shaped pin cushions and knick-knacks they had made for me.

And so, in spite of road noise, roaring planes, chanting soldiers, disturbed mental patients and rattling factories, life flowed on. As one of the staff remarked, "with the outside turmoil one has to have an inward serenity."

8. A New Arrival in Canton

Canton was a busy city. My bedroom window fronted one of the few wide roads, and because it led to the Governor's compound, the traffic was exceptionally heavy. Official cars, delegations and service personnel added to the constant stream of buses, vendors, rickshaws, heavily laden carts drawn by mangy horses or straining women, blind beggars, plodding water buffaloes, men with shoulder poles balancing baskets of vegetables, little boys herding a line of ducks, blaring cars and thousands of pedestrians.

Periodically a funeral procession would pass. The bereaved in white garments would be surrounded by professional wailers, and followed by papier mache chairs, tables and personal items to be burned at the grave side to accompany the dead soul into its afterlife. Sometimes a wedding procession would pass. The bride would be hidden behind curtains in a red chair, borne to the groom's house. Behind her would parade tables of dowry gifts.

After four in the afternoon, when the heat was slightly less oppressive, Miss Upsdell and I frequently went for a walk. The city was an ever-changing pageant, lively and interesting, but often pathetic and heart-wrenching.

"How can a mother exhibit her baby like that?" I complained one day as we passed a little child covered with suppurating sores, lying stretched out on the sidewalk as the mother begged.

"It attracts sympathy and gets a few pennies for food," replied my companion.

"Kumshah, kumshah, kumshah," clamoured the children, circling us with hands outstretched. We dared not give them anything or we never would have had a moment's peace.

I never got used to seeing young fellows snatch eagerly at cigarette stubs in the gutter to be recycled along with other stubs into a "new" cigarette.

"Hold your breath," we would warn one another. "Fish shop coming up." We hurried past to avoid the full impact of the yards of dried fish hanging on racks for sale.

Escaping from the confusion of the street and the sight of little children defecating in the gutters, we were relieved to turn into the cool confines of Blackwood Street. Canton had few wide roads in the thirties. Several main thoroughfares criss-crossed the city, but the narrow six-foot alleys led off to intriguing shops and historic places. One such lane I particularly liked was Blackwood Street. My parents had a number of pieces of the beautiful blackwood furniture in our home in Canada and I loved it, in spite of the fact that it had been my Saturday morning chore to dust and oil the huge, intricately carved desk.

We sauntered down the alley watching the workmen as they fitted the pieces together. The wood was so hard that no nails could be driven into it and no glue would hold it. Every part was carefully grooved and carved so the pieces would fit together exactly. The wood reminded me of the arbutus which grows on the west coast of British Columbia. The blackwood is gnarled and red before the black stain is put on, and it is fashioned into furniture for homes, particularly the more well-to-do establishments. Imperial palaces are full of examples of the more beautifully carved blackwood tables, chairs, screens, stools and even beds.

One could anticipate the next street by its aroma. I never ceased to marvel at the small boys who worked in Cedar Chest Lane. All down the alley, shaded by the buildings, sat urchins chipping away at designs etched on the chests by their elders. Figures of ancient heroes, flowering branches, birds and trees emerged as the youngsters chiselled nonchalantly. Father, uncle and grandfather hovered near at hand to advise, finish and polish. Carving a chest was a family affair.

Frequently at risk of spoiling our dinner, our walk would end with a feast of fried rice. I always found it difficult to pass the restaurant that specialized in my favourite Shrimp Chau Faan.

Some afternoons were spent farther afield. Each week the American mission compound — just a rickshaw ride away from our school — had open house for any friends who cared to drop in. Across the river the large American-supported University of Lingnam had a similar arrangement. Taking it in turn, the foreign staff opened their homes to their campus colleagues and to those of us who were more isolated and enjoyed a social afternoon. For the more energetic set, tea was usually followed by a fast-paced volleyball game. We played strenuously until the river ferry was in sight and then dashed for the dock, wiping the dripping perspiration from our faces.

As December approached, the thought of Christmas became uppermost in my mind. Christmas shopping for the folks at home had to be done early, as there was no airmail in those days and boat mail took weeks. With parcels dispatched and many letters written and mailed, we had time to plan activities.

Since China was not a Christian country, December 25 meant nothing to most people. However, Chiang Kai-shek, a nominal Christian, had conveniently announced that December 25 would be celebrated as Martyrs' Day in honour of some heroes who had fallen in defence of a cause. St. Hilda's, therefore, declared a few days holiday so that boarders would be able to enjoy a visit with their families. Several of the schoolgirls were daughters of Christian pastors in the villages and towns near Canton. Martyrs' Day gave them an opportunity to celebrate the Nativity with their families and in their local churches.

December weather is delightful in Canton, like warm June days at home. On Christmas Day, several of us young women connected with various missions, went on a hike and picnic to the White Cloud Hills outside Canton. In the evening, our own mission staff gathered for Christmas dinner, music and games at the Wittenbachs. A week later, 1932 passed into history, and I reflected on the events and experiences which had so changed my life.

But 1933 was to bring more momentous decisions. In late February the senior maths teacher, a Chinese woman graduate of Cambridge University, asked for three months maternity leave, beginning in early

April. The search for a suitable qualified replacement proved fruitless. Finally, my Principal asked me if I thought my fiance would consider accepting a short term appointment in a girls' school.

"I'm sure when he got out here he would find something by the fall term." she said. "Schools, in Hong Kong particularly, are always looking for replacements for staff going on furlough or even for permanent appointees."

With a thumping heart I assured her that I had no doubt he would be interested. She agreed to write to him with the terms of the agreement and ask for an immediate reply by cable.

It was a long three weeks for the Empress boat to sail to Vancouver with the letter, but eventually we received his cable of acceptance. Dick was to sail on the President line, leaving Seattle one week later. But because of the bitter strife of the depression years, the ship was sabotaged and sank in Seattle harbour. That meant a delay of a week when the Empress would sail from Vancouver.

Five weeks after his cable arrived I was in Hong Kong waiting impatiently for the big white Empress to dock. The fact that it sliced a junk in two in the fog and had to stop to search for survivors, prolonged the wait. Instead of a 7:00 a.m. arrival, it was 5:00 p.m. before the boat docked, leaving just enough time to move Dick's baggage to the night boat to Canton. In Canton Dick was accommodated in the Anglican Boys' School not far from St. Hilda's, and took his meals with the Wittenbachs.

The girls at the school were intrigued by a foreign male teacher, and Dick was equally intrigued with life in China. A few days after he arrived, the Chinese church was holding its annual dinner and the mission staff were all invited. Because Dick was a newcomer, he was the recipient of the customary Chinese hospitality and saw his bowl constantly supplemented by tidbits from the various dishes. After four or five courses, Dick, never a hearty eater, had reached his limit. The meal must surely be over, he thought. He was appalled as course followed course. Not realizing that fifteen or more courses would be served, he had graciously accepted the many choice morsels pressed on him by his hosts. It was a dinner — and a lesson — he never forgot.

Before long Dick was visiting the tailors and being fitted for tropical suits, but in spite of the lighter clothing he found the increasing heat oppressive. One day at the Wittenbachs he saw their baby lying almost naked in his crib and he noticed the little body covered with spots. Tactfully he asked Gertrude about the rash.

"Oh, that's just prickly heat," she said. "It's quite common."

Dick breathed a sigh of relief. When he had discovered his own rash he had wondered what dire tropical disease he had contracted.

Each morning when he left the boys' school, he passed a sentry box on a nearby corner. In the box was a clock, and one morning when his watch had stopped he decided to check the time. To see the clock he had to stoop slightly. The sentry immediately leapt to attention, shouldered his rifle and saluted, believing that Dick was bowing to him. Thereafter, every morning the sentry saluted and Dick obliged with a bow.

Once established in St. Hilda's, Dick began to inquire about appointments for the fall. Within a month he had three offers, including one from the Sun Yat Sen University in Canton. But Chinese university appointments were problematic, as they tended to be somewhat insecure and very dependent upon the political situation. He therefore accepted an offer from St. Stephen's Boys School in Hong Kong, replacing a teacher going on furlough for a year.

The next decision was about our summer holidays. It was necessary to get away from the heat of July and August, and a favourite holiday spot was a mountain on Lan Tau Island near Hong Kong. Various missions and some individuals had built permanent stone cottages on the mountain top, strong enough to resist typhoons. We applied for accommodation. I was able to share a two-room house with three other young women, and Dick found a place in a small unit with another young man.

Lan Tau was the choice of many South China missionaries. From Hong Kong, one caught a ferry to the island and then climbed to the top of the mountain with local coolies shouldering the luggage. The mission community had built a swimming pool in a shallow ravine which afforded excellent recreational facilities. Hikes across the peaks and into the valleys added to the fun and activity. A temple half-way down one of the nearby hills had overnight accommodation and a nearby waterfall for enjoyment and showers. A common mess house relieved campers from any responsibility for food preparation. Social activities and games created a relaxed and warm atmosphere and on Sundays the pulpit-table was decorated with mountain orchids gathered by the children.

By the end of August people began heading back to their various centres of work. I returned to Canton and St. Hilda's, and Dick went to Hong Kong and St. Stephen's Boys School. Dick's position was an interesting one. The boys had no common language. They came from Chinese communities throughout Asia: Malay, Indo-China, Indonesia and North China. The little fellows whom Dick shepherded were homesick like little boys in boarding schools anywhere. He had to help them adjust and to teach them English for communication amongst themselves as well as for their school subjects.

Meanwhile I was back with my senior classes, fortunately freed from teaching maths, which had previously taxed my non-mathematical mind. English text books were used, and the questions were asked in pounds, shillings and pence and English measurements.

On the way home from church one Sunday, some weeks later, several boarders invited me to come to their little sitting room in the evening. I was honoured. No foreign teacher went into the girls' room without an invitation and invitations were very rare. The girls were presenting some plays they had written themselves. They knew I wouldn't understand them as they were spoken in Chinese, but they assured me they would explain the stories to me. I looked forward with anticipation to the visit.

The Chinese seem to be born actors with a natural bent for improvisation and projection. I remembered the last school concert when the Grade nine's had improvised a play just a day before the presentation, and had the audience in stitches from beginning to end. There was no need for a written script. They produced an hilarious act with a "middle women" who arranged a marriage between a blind girl and a dumb man without either of the families knowing the disability of the other party. No inhibitions or lack of spontaneity restrained that cast!

At Christmas I had managed to get hold of a copy of Dickens' *A Christmas Carol* in play form, with the English script on one side and Chinese on the opposite page. It was an interesting experience to direct a play from an English script while the actors performed in Chinese. All went well, but on the day of the performance, the Cratchit's goose was a Chinese duck, pre-carved and put together as a whole on the platter. The cast sat down to eat. The dramatic conversation lasted only a page of two, but the duck was tasty and no one was inclined to leave the table before it was finished. So until the meal was properly disposed of, the characters kept up a lively impromptu patter which had the audience doubled up with laughter. I never did elicit from teachers or students a translation of the improvised conversation.

But the plays this Sunday evening were on a different plane. Caught up in the changing mores and the almost impassable generation gap, these girls were wrestling with moral and social problems that puzzled and disturbed them. Their questions were expressed in dramatic form.

One play depicted a young student, party to a marriage arranged by his family, who pursued his education and eventually went to America to study. There he met an educated Chinese girl whom he married. On his return to China he was confronted by his illiterate village wife and child. His dilemma was one of many being increasingly faced by the young people of the day. There were other issues: obedience to family versus the rights of an individual to control his or her own life, the place of an educated woman in Chinese society and the need for social reform. A great deal troubled the young people in the changing structures and mores of China in the thirties.

9. Changes, Decisions and a Wedding

Students everywhere were involved in changing social patterns, not only in the schools with revolutionary ideas. The Communists had been driven out of Canton in 1927, but Communist cells had sprung up everywhere. Rumours of activities were constantly circulating. We were told that one or two schools had been raided, and students had been arrested and never heard from since.

Walking down the main road one day I was dismayed to see a young man, bound and shackled, marched along the street by some soldiers. I suspected that he was a condemned Communist sympathizer. Ten minutes later, gunfire from the parade grounds near our school confirmed my suspicion that he had been taken to his execution.

That there was an undercurrent of unrest and desperation in the country was evident. There was constant talk of robbers in the hills and countryside. The authorities portrayed these malcontents as criminals. It became apparent, however, that the hopeless victims of repression and starvation were being driven to raiding villages and farms in order to survive. Banditry was now a way of life for thousands.

I have frequently been asked where Mao was at this time and if I had ever seen him in Canton. I had to admit that I was not aware of him. I look back with some degree of amazement at our ignorance of events. At the time, the foreign language papers gave little information; the picture was extremely confused.

After the Communists split with the Nationalists in 1927, they divided into two groups — those who went underground in Shanghai and kept contact with Moscow and those, led by Mao, who acted independently. When the government troops suppressed the 1927 Autumn Harvest Uprising, Mao and his followers went into the countryside in Hunan and Kiangsi provinces.

The group in Shanghai organized sabotage, strikes and uprisings in the cities. We heard about these events but the insurrections were always brutally put down by the army. All the while Mao was consolidating peasant support and creating soviet tenets far away from government control. News of his activity was vague. Often as not his followers were simply referred to as "bandits."

Mao was also far away from party headquarters. While internal squabbles were going on in Shanghai he was organizing peasants, starting a land revolution, dividing the land equally between rich and poor, and establishing self-sufficient communities in the hinterland. Although his supporters lived in incredibly poor conditions with negligible supplies and inadequate clothing, soldiers nevertheless deserted in large numbers from Chiang's army to join Mao. For months everyone lived on squash. According to Edgar Snow in his famous book *Red Star Over China*, soldiers rallied to the cry, "Down with capitalism and eat squash."

When government forces finally closed in on the Communist mountain hideouts, nearly a million people starved to death or were killed in Kwangsi province.

Life was not without danger for Mao himself. Once, while on an organizing tour, he was captured and taken to be executed at government army headquarters. Two hundred yards from the place of execution, he broke loose, running into the fields to hide in the tall grass. Strangely, soldiers and some peasants who had been forced to join the search failed to find him. When night came he escaped barefoot across the mountains, finding a friendly peasant to guide him to shelter.

In Canton, we heard only reports of civil war and uprisings. Canton itself was relatively quiet. In fact, some of the better aspects of Chiang's policies were having some effect. Under the banner of "The New Life Movement," attempts were made to increase educational opportunities.

A train coach was equipped with instructional films on health and public sanitation and was dropped off at towns and villages along the railway lines for community presentations.

Young people were eager to do something. Chiang Kai-shek became a popular figure and large "Chiang" buttons appeared on coat lapels and dresses. Dick had to come to terms with his class. Every time Chiang Kai-shek's name was mentioned, the whole class would leap to their feet and stand at attention. Eventually Dick was able to persuade the students to observe this ritual only on formal occasions.

The emphasis on education and public health encouraged students to take action. Some of the St. Hilda's girls requested permission for weekend absence to go to the countryside to give addresses on sanitation and health. Other students carried on weekend and holiday classes for the illiterate street urchins in the vicinity of the school.

"They're sitting on our doorstep at six o'clock in the morning wanting to know when school starts," complained one of the servants, who nearly fell over a small child sitting there practising characters on a slate.

"China needs a million new school teachers," said Chiang. We applauded, wondering at the same time where the training facilities were. "Before this problem is solved," he announced, "China must have a national language." So all our graduates went off to night school to study Mandarin.

But pronouncements were one thing; achievements, another. Some improvements were made in the fields of finance, communications, defence and light industry. The failure to carry out social and economic reform was fatal, however. The October 1928 provisional constitution had outlined a progressive six-year program of training for the nation, in order to teach people how to vote, an unheard of privilege. Eager to see a democratic China, we waited for elections which never came, or even for some evidence of preparatory training which never materialized. Reconstruction was spasmodic and totally inadequate.

On the surface it appeared as if unity and stability might be achieved in China. But Chiang offered only lip service to Sun Yat-sen's Three Principles.

We were distressed when a young American couple arrived from the interior distraught and bitter. The mission where they worked had run a leper colony for many years. People suffering from leprosy were encouraged to come to the village, give their healthy children into the hands of those who would care for them in a nearby school, and take treatment and therapy themselves. Gradually, confidence had been built up as more and more lepers gathered in the centre for help.

Recently, a group of soldiers from Chiang's army had arrived at the village and announced that the government had arranged to give these unfortunate people fifty cents a day. News spread and more patients arrived. Then, one day at noon, as the lepers gathered for their dole, the soldiers raised their guns and massacred them. Needless to say, other leper colonies dissolved and the disease spread. Another blow had been struck against social reform and reconstruction.

By March 1934, our thoughts turned to summer vacation. Some of the foreign community discussed the possibility of holidaying on one of the mountain peaks in South China. With Mao and his followers pushed into the hinterland, the so-called brigands had been temporarily routed. It was now considered safe to venture to beautiful Loh Fau Mountain, half way between Canton and Hong Kong. There were no permanent buildings there, but Europeans and Americans, along with a sprinkling of Chinese friends, contracted for the building of mat sheds at the 5,000 foot level. By the summer, these native huts were built, furnished simply and were ready for our use.

We travelled down river by small boats, walked across the paddy fields, stayed overnight in a Buddhist temple, and in the morning climbed to the heights. Although we were in the clouds for four of the six weeks, the fun and fellowship made up for the chilly fog.

Much of the fresh food for the camp mess was purchased in the villages at the foot of the mountain. But the villagers refused to accept paper money. It had on it the signature of the government, and who could tell how long the current government would last? Consequently silver was the only acceptable currency, and since the only silver coin was a twenty-cent piece, we all had to carry one hundred dollars each in twenty-cent pieces with us up the mountain.

September saw Dick and me back at school again. Dick's year as substitute teacher at St. Stephen's had been completed, but he had received a permanent appointment at Ying Wa Boys' School in Kowloon run by the London Missionary Society. We looked forward to the end of our separation by the following summer, and settled ourselves down for a ten-month stint. But 1934 had surprises for us.

St Hilda's was badly in need of repairs. The old buildings that housed the school boarders were becoming untenable. We could not face another rainy season with the roofs in such poor conditions. One of my letters to my family in Vancouver, dated May 13, 1934, reads:

> I wish you could see 91 Paak Tze Lo and environs today! It has been raining without ceasing for the last sixteen hours, and I can't describe the situation. This place leaks like a sieve.
>
> Miss Upsdell didn't get to sleep last night till 4 a.m. because of the terrible rain. Finally she had to get up and put a mackintosh over her mosquito net. Miss Wong, one of the teachers, got rained out of her room in the night and had to move in to her little sister's bed in the girls' dormitory. We have to use umbrellas everywhere we go in the buildings, and had to move into the Abbot's bedroom for lunch as the water was pouring all around our feet and even on to the table. The bedroom wasn't much better. In the sitting room we have a bucket or two to catch the drips.
>
> It is at a time like this that we wish our dear friends who exclaim, "what a lovely, picturesque compound this is," would arrive for a visit. We've caught so many buckets of rainwater already that we don't know what to do with it.

The Mission owned property not far away on a pleasant road leading to the White Cloud Hills, where a modern school for boys had been built. The Mission Secretary made a proposal that St. Hilda's be sold and the money used to build on the property adjoining the boys' school.

Everyone rejoiced, and the plans were put into action. But we were not prepared for the deviousness of the authorities. They offered the explanation that the municipality — annoyed with the Buddhists for selling their property to the foreigners — had neglected to give the Mission the one small all-important document which would permit re-sale. As long as the school remained there, nothing was done, but it could not be sold. The only answer was to close the school.

The depression had dried up all funds from home churches. The sale of the property had been the only answer to a new school. An air of gloom settled over the school. The students knew that there was no other school offering the English training available at St. Hilda's. Many of our graduates entered the Nursing School of the British Government Hospital in Hong Kong. They were not required to take the English language entrance exams because our graduation standards were acceptable. Other students of St. Hilda's became teachers, and their qualifications in English assisted them in getting positions. Chinese government regulations had been promulgated, which ordered all teaching was to be done in Chinese, but St. Hilda's principal had ignored the directive. The school's programme was unique.

It was a sad time for all of us — staff, students and servants alike. But there was no alternative, and the decision was made to close the school. As of December 1934, St. Hilda's School would cease to exist.

Although I had a year to run on my contract and would miss the friends I had made among both staff and students, there was a bright side to the story for me personally. Dick and I would be able to marry by Christmas, 1934.

Planning a Canton wedding was an intriguing experience. Either one invited a few intimate friends or practically the whole of the mission community in and around the city, as well as the school staff and senior girls. Since none of our family would be present, we elected for the latter, and sent out more than 120 invitations.

The week before Christmas was as pleasant a time as one could find in tropical Canton. The day turned out to be like a beautiful June day at home. A New Zealand couple who had been close friends of my parents acted on their behalf, and the wedding party was a cosmopolitan group of Americans, New Zealanders, Australians and British, with an exchange student from Vancouver as best man.

The wedding cake was ordered from a Chinese bakery but they disclaimed any knowledge of almond paste for the icing. Consequently the girls and I had a hilarious time grinding almonds in the school kitchen and making the icing. When we delivered it to the bakery we found that almond paste, under another name, was already included on the cake, so we had a double layer.

On our wedding morning, Dick and the bridesmaids went to the flower market at 6:00 a.m., and for about two dollars Canadian, purchased armfuls of yellow, white and golden chrysanthemums — enough for all the bouquets and church decorations.

While the staff and bridesmaids made up the bouquets and decorated, Dick and I went to the British Consulate at 10:00 a.m. on December 18, where the official knot was tied. Whilst the church ceremony at 2:00 p.m. was a much more meaningful service, it was legally unessential. Dick has frequently baffled friends over the years by telling them that both of us have been married twice.

Since we had regularly attended the English-speaking services in Union Church on the island of Shameen, the wedding was held there. I dressed for the occasion in the same house on Shameen that my mother had used on her wedding day. Since no vehicles were permitted on the small island, I was carried to the church in a sedan chair.

After the ceremony, we crossed the river in small motor boats and held the reception in the poinsettia-encircled garden of the New Zealand Presbyterian Mission.

Our honeymoon was spent on a cruise aboard an Empress liner to the Philippines. In the thirties, the *Empresses of Asia, Russia, Canada* and *Japan* plied fortnightly between Vancouver and Manila. Calling at Hong Kong, they then sailed for Manila, stopped over for three days and paid a return call at Hong Kong. Christmas day saw us shooting the rapids on the river to Pagsanjan Falls, and the remaining days enjoying the tropical beauty of the Philippine Islands.

10. Build up to Revolution

Although we were now living in Hong Kong, events in China influenced our daily lives. Ninety-eight percent of the population of Hong Kong was Chinese and most people had relatives living on the mainland. As our closest friends remained in Canton, we frequently visited the city. Naturally, events in China concerned us deeply.

Chiang Kai-shek was still regarded as the hope of the nation and the Communists as a disruptive element destroying unity. News reports chiefly referred to them as "the bandits in the hills." Looking back, I still marvel at how uninformed we were of the events taking place.

In October 1934, the Communists were nearly surrounded. Quickly and secretly they managed to evacuate their base in the Chingkang Mountains. Loading factory equipment and ammunition on to mules and donkeys, they organized the army units — and all the peasants who wanted to go with them — and started off. When the enemy followed, they circled and changed directions, but continued to move north west. Because of terrible hardships and bombing attacks, thousands died or were forced to give up and settle in villages along the way.

To reach the westerly province of Szechuan, they had to cross the Tatu River, which was narrow, deep and swift. When the marchers arrived at the only fordable place, the enemy was waiting on the other side with bombers flying overhead. A quick decision was made. They would move 130 miles west, where a famous iron-chain bridge crossed a deep gorge.

They started off barefooted up and down the steep banks in a race with the Nationalists on the opposite side. Chiang's troops, believing that the Red Army could not travel in the difficult terrain at great speed, and assuming they would rest at night, camped each night. But the Communists did not stop. They reached the bridge to find that only a small local detachment was covering it with machine guns.

Thick boards usually lashed over the chains had been removed from the marchers' side of the bridge. A call for volunteers went out to dare the impossible. Of the many who eagerly came forward, thirty young men under twenty-five years of age were chosen. In spite of the enemy snipers who sent some into the boiling river below, more than twenty swung across the chains, reached the flooring and raced across, throwing hand grenades into the enemy machine-gun nest.

"Long live the thirty heroes of Tatu Ho" screamed the marchers, as the daring men carried out their incredible feat. By the time the Nationalist army reached the bridge the local detachment had retreated, the Red Army had crossed and was on its way into Szechuan province.

But another 2,000 miles — across seven mountain ranges, some of them 16,000 feet high — still lay before the straggling army. They crossed swampland, met wild tribes in the mountains and suffered severe exhaustion. But eventually 20,000 of the 90,000 armed men, with a few women and the peasants who had joined them, survived, arriving in northern Shensi province in late 1935, after 369 days of marching. They had passed through twelve provinces, crossed eighteen mountain ranges and twenty-four rivers, broken through the armies of ten different war lords, and averaged twenty-four miles a day with all their transport and people, over some of the most dangerous trails on earth. It has been called the greatest mass migration in history.

Many had died along the way and some had stayed in the cities and villages through which the army had passed. In every area they went through, the Red Army held mass meetings and left organizers to train the people. Some of the marchers stayed behind as workers so there would be Communist bases everywhere along the line. Men in the villages joined up to take their places. Mao, expressing himself in classical verse form, wrote:

The Red Army fears not the trials of the Long March
Holding light ten thousand crags and torrents.

The Five Ridges wind like gentle ripples
And the majestic Wumeng roll by, globules of clay.
Warm the steep cliffs lapped by the waters of Gold Sand,
Cold the iron chains spanning the Tatu River.
Minshan's thousand li of snow joyously crossed,
The three Armies march on, each face glowing.

Unbelievably, we in Hong Kong knew nothing of this courageous journey until historians recorded it years later.

By the time the remnant of the marchers reached the northwest, Mao had established himself as the undisputed leader. He began to rebuild the party, to initiate reforms and to mobilize the populace. By 1936, he had set up his headquarters in Yenan and had begun to organize the Chinese People's Soviet Republic. There was now a price on his head.

"A quarter of a million dollars for the capture of Mao," offered Chiang in desperation. Still Mao walked freely among the peasants: although many were starving, no one took up the offer. Mao forbade his troops to exploit the people like the Nationalist troops did. I have seen copies of the rules laid down for the Communist soldiers. The People's Liberation Army memorized those rules and they were incorporated into a Red Army song. They said:

1. Prompt obedience to orders
2. No confiscation whatever from the poor peasants
3. Prompt delivery directly to the Government for its disposal of all goods confiscated from the landlords
4. Replace all doors when you leave a house
5. Return and roll up the straw matting on which you sleep
6. Be courteous and polite to the people and help them when you can
7. Return all borrowed articles
8. Replace all damaged articles
9. Be honest in all transactions with the peasants
10. Pay for all articles purchased
11. Be sanitary, and especially establish latrines a safe distance from people's houses

When I first read these rules, the fourth one mystified me. Why the regulation about replacing doors? "Because," explained a Chinese man, "the wooden doors on a Chinese house are easy to take off. Sometimes they are taken down at night, put on wooden blocks and used for a bed. The peasants would often make up a bed for a soldier in this way."

Discussing the passage of troops through West China, a friend of mine who lived in that area said, "When Chiang Kai-shek's men came into our town they would come to our school and demand the use of the girls' dormitory. We would have to crowd the students into another part of the school and watch very carefully that the girls were not molested. The troops sometimes stabled their horses in our dining hall and they looted the local stores for supplies.

"When the people first heard the Communists were coming they were terrified. The Communist command also came to our school but asked politely for permission to use the premises. They made no advances to the students. They kept the place very clean and they paid the storekeepers and farmers for everything. They often helped the people with their work or the harvesting. Is it any wonder the people supported them?"

Meanwhile Chiang Kai-shek was plagued by the Communist challenge, the growing menace of Japan, and the need for reform. Economic conditions were appalling and the suffering of the people was beyond belief.

"Did you ever wonder where your word 'shanghaied' came from?" a Chinese teacher, Mr. Chen, asked me one day. I had to admit I hadn't given it much thought. "I'll tell you," he said. "Someone would come from Dairen or one of the other northern ports and recruit dock workers in Shanghai. Men would be seized and forced to go to the harbour cities. Their lives were, as we say, 'worse than that of a horse or an ox.' Sixty dock workers would live in one room and in the winter the water froze in the basin. Roofs were so low that the workers could hardly stand up. They were packed so tightly they could only roll over in bed together. They worked fifteen hours a day, and every day someone died from hunger, accident or illness."

The word 'shanghaied' took on new meaning for me.

"At one point," Mr. Chen added, "out of 3,000 dock workers taken from Shanghai, 2,900 of them died within a year. Then they would come back and seize a few thousand more."

In an attempt to improve the lot of the Chinese people, Chiang inaugurated the New Life Movement. Postage stamps incorporated in each corner the Confucian characters for politeness, integrity, self-respect and righteousness. Outwardly Chiang tried to insist on government integrity, but the practice of "squeeze" was endemic in the system. Government servants paid no attention to admonitions.

"The Kuomintang was the biggest speculator in drugs," Mr. Chen insisted. "The head of the police bureau in Shanghai was a drug speculator. He had a factory in Hongshu producing drugs. He pretended to support drug prevention, but the common saying was, 'if you're arrested for drugs at the front door of the police station, you're released at the back door.'" Platitudes were not the answer to China's needs. Young people were demanding education and government resistance to Japan. Economic and social conditions cried out for basic reform.

When we visited Canton over Christmas in 1935, students were demonstrating against Nanking's passive attitude to Japan. They waylaid buses and cars and a few free-for-alls took place. One or two volleys of shots were fired to disperse excited mobs. Schools were shut down to prevent students from congregating and organizing. It became dangerous to speak out.

As we sat talking to our friends one afternoon, we heard anxious voices and the sound of sobbing. The servant brought in a hysterical young woman.

"Wai Ling, what is the matter?" our friends asked, as they held the distraught girl. "What has happened?"

"My brother," she gasped. "They've shot him."

"Who shot him?"

"The soldiers."

"Why?"

"He was talking to his friends in a tea shop a few days ago. He said something against the government." Her voice broke. "Spies heard him. He was arrested yesterday. This morning they took him to the execution grounds and shot him."

"Do your parents know?"

"I don't think so . . . .He was their only son . . . I must go to them," and she stumbled from the room still sobbing. We sat in stunned silence. The life of that promising student had been snuffed out for an unguarded remark.

"The South is getting restive," our friends commented. "There is a secession movement that is threatening to disrupt what unity Chiang has achieved. An Anti-Japanese Salvation Army has been organized to resist the Japanese invasion."

Returning to Hong Kong we watched, with growing concern, the opposing forces. Chiang Kai-shek wanted to finish off the Communists and ordered attacks on their positions in the northwest. But his officers and men were sick of civil war and were becoming sympathetic to demands for a united front to fight Japan.

Finally in December 1936, Chiang flew to Sian to see Chang Hsueh-liang and Yang Hu-ch'eng, two of his commanders, in an effort to organize the campaign against the Communists. A mutiny erupted, however, engineered by the forces of the two commanders. Chiang was held captive. The young Marshall Chang made eight demands:

1. A united front
2. An end to civil war
3. Freedom for all patriots arrested in Shanghai
4. Release of political prisoners
5. Right of assembly
6. Right to organize a patriotic movement
7. Promotion of Sun Yat-sen's Three Principles
8. Immediate calling of a National Salvation Conference

News of the kidnapping of Chiang stunned the world. We envisioned the outbreak of a more vicious civil war. Japan gloated, since a weakened China was to her great advantage. Nanking sent airplanes. A punitive expedition was planned. But both Communists and Warlords knew that disorder would play into Japan's hands. At this point, Chou En-lai emerged as a mediator. We waited for news.

On Christmas Day, 1936, as we were sitting down to dinner, we were startled by a thunderous barrage of fire crackers. Chiang had been released on the promise that he would form a united front with the Communists against Japan. Hong Kong went wild.

The effect on Japan was immediate. Anxious to continue her incursions into China, encouraged by the ease with which she had conquered Manchuria and delighted with the failure of the League of Nations to support sanctions, Japan began to plan for the strengthening of her hold on north China. In February 1937, an army coup in Tokyo established the militarists solidly in power in Japan. But conditions in China had been unstable for so many years that foreigners did not consider the situation any more dangerous than usual.

As we discussed our summer holidays with friends, someone remarked, "This is the year to visit Japan. The drop in the value of the yen makes holidays there financially attractive."

"Let's go to Korea," someone else suggested. "Wonsan Beach is beautiful. We can rent a house there very reasonably." This idea was greeted with enthusiasm and so it was decided.

We were fortunate enough to get a large house big enough for our friends, their two young boys, Dick, myself and our year-old son David. We embarked on our trip little suspecting what would happen in the next month.

11. Korean Holiday

Korea at this time was a dependency of Japan and completely under her control. Japanese currency was used throughout the country. To reach Korea, it was necessary for us to go through Japan, so in July 1937, we set sail for Kobe.

The Japanese were courteous but unbending and completely lacking in any sense of humour. We had been warned not to crack any jokes. Just do what they say, we were told.

Knowing that China's weakness was to her benefit, Japan had continued to foster disorder on an enfeebled population. At the same time, she poured into China settlers from Japan and adopted the Russian tactic of sending in military personnel disguised as railway guards. Korea was the connecting link, and the highway from Japan to north China had excellent train service throughout. Our trip through Japan — across the straits by boat, and by train again to Wonsan — was quick, efficient and without incident.

In Korea strict censorship was enforced, and propaganda had brainwashed even the foreign communities into believing that Japan was "saving China" and helping her to build up the industrial north. Foreigners nevertheless were aware of suppression because their magazines were arriving with ads and articles removed, and mail from overseas was constantly censored.

Chatting with four members of the foreign community in Korea, we heard some amusing but disturbing stories. "I wrote a letter home," one missionary told us, "and I warned my family that our letters were opened and censored." She began to laugh. "Half an hour after the letter was posted, a policeman arrived at my door to assure me that foreigners' mail was never opened and read."

"I received a report from our mission secretary the other day," an Australian added. "Enclosed was a complete Japanese translation inadvertently included when the letter was resealed."

"When our Jeremy was passing the post office," his wife added, "he was called into the head office. As he speaks fluent Japanese, he was asked to translate a letter. Coincidentally the letter happened to be from one official to another in his father's mission."

No one in Japan or Korea was allowed to have a short-wave radio, and noise transmissions were sent out to drown Russian and Chinese stations. Japanese people were taught that they were saving China so she could stand with Japan in reclaiming "Asia for the Asiatics." The movement of foreigners was strictly curtailed. Everyone had to inform the local constabulary of any impending journeys no matter how short.

One of our Australian friends had served at one time in the British intelligence service. The Japanese, examining a snapshot album included among his books when he arrived in Japan, discovered a picture of him in uniform. From then on he was a marked man. In addition, he was an artist employed by the missionary press to produce illustrations for their literature. As his home happened to be in a militarized zone, his every move was followed by the police and his sketching activities were closely watched. One Monday, half an hour after he had posted a letter to his wife at Wonsan Beach, the police were at his door.

"You are leaving on Wednesday for Wonsan?" they asked.

"Yes."

"You are catching the train at noon?"

"Right."

"You will not leave this house for the next two days without our permission."

From Monday to Wednesday, a police officer sat on our friend's porch, finally escorting him to the train where he was turned over to another officer who accompanied him on the five hour train trip to Wonsan.

While we vacationed at Wonsan Beach, police were on duty at all times to oversee activities. Groups of more than half a dozen were not allowed to meet without the attendance of a policeman. The Canadian Mission held its annual meetings at the beach and the policeman sat through all the proceedings. A previous pronouncement had forbidden the singing of the hymn "Work For the Night is Coming," because of its ominous sound.

But in spite of the surveillance, the holiday was a delightful experience. The warm ocean rolled in over a beautiful beach of fine white sand; there was fun and fellowship with predominantly Canadian and Australian missionary families, and a three-day walking trip through the spectacular Diamond Mountains provided excitement and change. The Diamond Mountains are so-called because they are full of crystal which is cut and polished into beautiful jewellery and decorative articles. On the first day of our visit, we climbed to the top of Bambutsuso, literally translated "The Aspect of Myriad Things." It is supposed that the fantastic jagged rock formations represent all things existing in the world.

The climb was so strenuous in parts that chains were fastened for climbers to pull themselves up. Ladders and irregular stone steps numbering 1,043, covered half the distance. The view from the top was the reward; the scramble along the jagged crags, exhilarating.

We spent the second day at sea level, boating between the rocky projections and diving for fascinating shells in the crystal clear water. Our final day was climaxed by a visit to the Nine Dragon Falls where the water dropped 150 feet over sheer rock into bubbling pools. Here we were able to swim and listen to some charming local legends.

One of the delights of the trip was making the acquaintance of Pastor Yhun who supported himself and his work by running a Korean Inn for travellers. He spoke good English and regaled us with many tales. My favourite concerned Creation:

> After Creation the donkey came to the Heavenly Father and said, "Heavenly Father, why was I created?"
>
> "That you might carry men's burdens and work for them."
>
> "And how many years am I to live?"
>
> "Thirty years, the same as man." "But Heavenly Father, I don't want to live so long — only ten years."

So the Heavenly Father granted his request. Then came the dog with the same questions and the Heavenly Father said to him, "You are to guard man and to watch and protect the young for thirty years."

"But Father, I wish to live only ten years," said the dog. His request was also granted.

Next came the monkey seeking the same answers. "You are to amuse man and to be funny and foolish." Again the request was for ten years only and the Father granted it.

Finally man came and he was told, "You are to enjoy yourself, but your chief purpose is to love and serve God."

"And how long may I live?"

"Thirty years."

"But Father, that is not long enough for life is good and I would like to serve you longer."

"Then you may have the extra twenty years of the donkey and after your first thirty years of joy and freedom you shall work hard for twenty years carrying the burdens of life from thirty to fifty."

"But Heavenly Father, fifty years is not enough. Pray grant more," pleaded the man.

"Then you may have the years of the dog and from fifty to seventy you must watch over your grandchildren and over the home and guard and protect them."

"Thank you, Heavenly Father, but grant still longer."

"Then take the twenty years of the monkey and from seventy to ninety you will look like him for your teeth will fall out and you will be foolish and amusing."

And so man was satisfied and his days are as fourscore and ten.

But while we were enjoying a vacation in Japanese-dominated Korea, events in China were moving to a showdown. A Japanese garrison in North China undertook some manoeuvres just outside Peking, near the Marco Polo Bridge in July 1937. On the pretext of searching for a supposedly missing soldier, the Japanese military demanded the right to enter the city. When the Chinese commander refused the request, the city was bombarded and occupied. An undeclared war had been launched.

"It will be over in a month," an American dentist in Korea assured us. "The Chinese will never be able to stand up to the crack Japanese army." In later years I wished that I had met this gentleman again in 1945.

Troop trains began pouring through north Korea on the way to China. The Japanese military allowed three months for the conclusion of the war. Japanese newspapers, the only source of our news, reported battles with two thousand Chinese dead, four Japanese killed and twenty-four wounded.

China mobilized. The Communists, the Kuomintang and the students all united in the face of a struggle for national survival. To avoid the destruction of its priceless treasures, Peking was evacuated in late July. By the end of the month, Tientsin had fallen.

Some of the foreigners holidaying at Wonsan decided to leave for home, but we elected to stay as we had reservations on the President liner for the end of August. And so we watched and waited.

12. *Hazards of War*

While we stayed on at Wonsan Beach, the Japanese attacked Shanghai. The city was the financial and economic centre of China, where support for the war would be crucial to China's cause. Chiang Kai-shek was able to hold back the advance for three months with his German-trained divisions.

Towards the end of August we crossed the Korean Straits and boarded a train for the scenic trip along the shores of the Japanese Inland Sea to Kobe. War fever was rampant. Women in kimonos were standing on street corners soliciting funds and encouraging people to take down iron gates and metal constructions of any sort, to donate the metal to the war effort. Store radios blared "It's a Long Way to Tipperary," and "Pack up your Troubles" with Japanese words. Passers-by were encouraged to stitch lucky knots into wraps for the soldiers. Our train coaches waited on sidings while troop trains were rushed through. We were fortunate in getting the last rooms in an inn in Kobe. With people returning from furloughs and holidays, Japan was overflowing with those trying to get to various destinations. Except for a relatively small field in south China, Shanghai was the point of disembarkation for the whole of China. But Shanghai was under seige. Japan, Hong Kong and Manila were teeming with travellers.

Three President and two Empress liners, as well as British, German and French ships, had been going back and forth evacuating foreigners from Shanghai. We were scheduled to pick up more refugees. As our ship neared the mouth of the river leading to the city, searchlights played over us. At 3:00 a.m. we anchored, and at 8:00 a.m. we started up the river, followed by an American gunboat. Then suddenly we found a small Japanese gunboat riding alongside, under cover of our ship. We could see the Chinese soldiers in their trenches along the banks, but they did not fire for fear of hitting an American ship. Finally, the Japanese boat made a run and the fire opened up.

A distraught officer kept appearing on deck, saying, "Please return to the lounge. It is dangerous on deck."

Everyone would retreat, but the curious were soon out to watch again. One or two shells whistled over our boat, but we felt reasonably safe as we assured each other that neither the Japanese nor the Chinese would attack an American boat. We had placed American flags all over the ship, and a huge one was spread out on the deck for the benefit of airplanes overhead.

Hundred of refugees were waiting in the city to be evacuated. The *President Taft* had just sailed with people sleeping on couches in the lounge, and the *Empress of Asia* had left with 1,400 people on board with queues for meals and mattresses on the decks. Families were frantically trying to locate other members who had been separated during holidays. Some foreign casualties had been reported in Shanghai as a result of the Japanese bombing.

As the Japanese gunboat eased past us, firing began in earnest. A battle raged while we sat on one side of it and the lighter, bearing the refugees for our ship, sat on the other.

Suddenly there was a scream of diabolical glee and someone shrieked, "They've got it! She's going down." We all rushed to the window as a Japanese plane, hit by a Chinese anti-aircraft gun, plunged into the river only 500 yards upstream from our ship.

The destruction of the plane was the signal for an all-out bombing attack, and we watched as Japanese planes rose like flies and rained missiles down on the anti-aircraft nests. More Japanese gunboats angled in close to us so the Chinese could not fire without hitting the President liner.

When the smoke and the noise finally cleared, the lighter deposited the weary refugees and we hightailed it for the river mouth. We met the *President Hoover* coming up from Hong Kong, the last boat to go into Shanghai.

When we arrived in Hong Kong we were confronted with newspaper headlines, "*President* arrives bullet-ridden from Shanghai." We were rather amused and assured our friends that the best we could offer were a few pock-marks from rifle shots. But when the news came of the bombing of the *President Hoover*, we realized the hazardous position we had been in. A bomb, fortunately a dud, was dropped down the *Hoover's funnel*. Further calls were now too dangerous. Hong Kong was brimming over, and like everyone else, we opened our home to those who could not find a place to stay. We hosted two British businesswomen who finally returned to Shanghai once the Japanese gained control and business began to carry on again.

Missionaries from West China, who normally spent six weeks going by steamer from Shanghai up the Yangtze Gorges to Chungking, were now flying to West China from Hong Kong in six hours. Two or three of the men of the party would take the baggage by boat, train and truck to Indo-China and through Yunnan into Chengdu.

From Toronto, we received requests for rooms for United Church missionaries returning to West China. We gladly shared our home with an interesting stream of visitors. Probably the most unusual guest was Mr. Davidson, head of the Agricultural College of West China Union University. In an attempt to upgrade egg and poultry production, he planned to cross breed the hardy little Chinese chicken with a heavy egg-producing Canadian breed. While in Vancouver, he procured two hens and a rooster from the outstanding flocks developed at the University of British Columbia. Hen number six had been a star performer, world record breaker and the subject of innumerable jokes and conjectures during our university days. The department had continued to breed outstanding strains.

When the ship docked in Hong Kong, Mr. Davidson produced his livestock, and we penned them on the roof of our apartment. The Chinese were staggered. Never had they seen such birds. Beside the little twelve-inch Chinese fowl, the cock — fully thirty-six inches from beak to tail tip — was a monster. A steady stream of sightseers was conducted by our fascinated amahs up the back stairs to the roof. The cock's vociferous crowing at daybreak sounded far and wide and brought a tearful reaction from our little one-year-old son.

Meanwhile, the Japanese continued to advance. Outflanking the Chinese forces they moved south, and in mid-December the capital, Nanking, fell. The "rape of Nanking" became a byword. Foreigners who had escaped from the city brought tales of horror and destruction. Even the Japanese authorities kept their actions concealed from their own people.

When Tokyo offered Chiang harsh terms for capitulation, he refused. He moved his capital to Chungking in the western province of Szechuan, whose geographical features made enemy penetration almost impossible. In the spring of 1938, a heroic stand at T'ai-erh Chuang in North China gave the Chinese a major victory, after which they opened the dykes of the Yellow River to slow the Japanese advance.

In Hong Kong, we were shocked by the burning and shelling of Chinese fishing junks by the Japanese in British waters. Hardly aware that there was a war, hundreds of fishermen lost their lives; the lucky ones lost only their boats. Fishboats then refused to go to sea, and the price of fish — a staple food in the colony — rose dramatically.

Bombers were now overhead in Canton. Our friends moved their wives and children to Hong Kong, although the men themselves returned to work. Mission hospitals worked around the clock, but were frequently the target for attack. The railways from Hong Kong to Canton and on to Hankow, though frequently bombed, miraculously kept pushing supplies into the interior. Every garage in Hong Kong was assembling diesel army trucks imported from Europe, while the road crews rushed through the new highway from the British colony to Canton.

Foreign children and many business people were evacuated from cities in the path of the Japanese advance. But many foreigners stayed behind to maintain a "safety zone" for the stricken people in the captured cities. The boys in our school, most of them from relatively poor families, raised over a thousand dollars by selling subscriptions and cards and organizing concerts. The money went to national salvation bonds which were used by relief committees caring for the thousands of refugees who poured into the city.

One of our teachers reported that a friend had sent word of 7,000 wounded soldiers lying on the waterfront road in Nanking with nothing whatever to protect them from the winter weather and no doctor or nurse available. Christian organizations and students were doing their best to alleviate some of the suffering. But they could offer little medical help. Few Hong Kong doctors volunteered their services and were strongly criticized for their selfishness.

Naturally, schools were deeply affected by the war. In China, whole institutions were moved either to Hong Kong or far into the interior.

"Our comparatively simple life of a few years ago has gone," commented one West China worker. "We have crowds of students and professors from down river on our campus. The left wing, of course, is very strong amongst the student class and they are afraid of Chiang suing for peace. Consequently they have been very active and go out at weekends to instruct the country folk in guerrilla warfare."

One criticism, levelled by an American bishop, is interesting in the light of post-war developments in China. "So far," he said, "the war had been fought by the lower classes, the villagers and the coolies. The upper classes have not yet realized that, unless they take the lead and support their country, China must fail."

When we asked the Bishop what the response was to his criticism, he said that they had excused themselves by claiming that they hadn't been called on yet. "'The villagers can do it,' they said, 'and then after they have finished, the citizens may be called to do something.'"

Yes, we agreed. The well-to-do and the educated were making their quiet get-away to Hong Kong or abroad, leaving the poorer folk to face the conflict.

"It's old China," the Bishop reflected, "and I had hoped it was gone."

Here lay the seeds of the Revolution. The leadership of China was forfeited by the privileged. It fell to the peasants and workers to restore the nation in the years to come.

13. Return to Canada

"I hate these moonlit nights," I said to my husband as we stood on our apartment verandah looking out towards the hills separating the British Territories from South China. "It means the Japanese bombers will be out in full force."

It was a beautiful evening in January 1938. The war had now reached the south with bombing raids. We had read in the paper that a bomb had landed twenty feet in front of the hospital at Kong Chuen, killing one of the attendants. I thought of one of my bridesmaids whose husband was a doctor. She had been sent to Hong Kong but he was still in Canton and had written to say that he was often operating with glass flying and plaster falling.

We listened for the distant sound of planes. I wondered how soon it would be before the Japanese invaded the south. The British were strengthening their defence in the hills around the New Territories. There were twice as many troops in Hong Kong as there had been. Trial blackouts made us very aware of the need for preparation. Severe fines of a thousand dollars were imposed on anyone showing an uncovered light.

Hong Kong was more crowded and busier than ever. Not only were refugees pouring into the colony, but it was becoming the crossroads of the East. The loss of Shanghai gave added importance to Hong Kong as a coordinating centre for freight, relief work and business.

At this time Canada made a contribution in China's hour of need in the person of Dr. Norman Bethune. Although he spent only eighteen months in China, Dr. Bethune is a living legend there. On his death in November 1939, from septicaemia, his Chinese comrades said, "not in all China, no, not in all the world will there be enough tears." In a year and a half, he transformed the medical services of the Communist-held areas, wrote medical texts, trained personnel and tended the wounded night and day. His sacrificial devotion still inspires the people of China, and his picture hangs in countless halls and homes throughout the country.

While the Red Army in North China was harassing the Japanese, the enemy's southern contingent was moving slowly down the coast. As more cities fell, our own future was deeply affected. Chinese families who could afford to go, were leaving Hong Kong, fearful of the future. Others were moving back to ancestral homes deep in the interior. With the withdrawal of students and the demands of war, school finances became difficult.

"I'm afraid that after your furlough in 1939," Dick was told, "it is unlikely that we will be able to afford to maintain you on staff." This was a blow. We enjoyed our work in Hong Kong and had anticipated a permanent appointment.

In Japan the great Christian and social reformer, Dr. Kagawa, called for an end to the war with China. At one of his packed meetings he stood for a long time with bowed head and then said, "This is not Kagawa standing here. It is but his shadow. The real Kagawa is over there in China with the suffering mothers and Chinese multitude made homeless by the war."

Along with this story, his poem "To Tears" was circulated in a private communication from Christians in Japan:

Ah tears! Unbidden tears!
Familiar friends since childhood's lonely years,
Long separated we,
Why do you come again to dwell with me?

At midnight, dawn, midday
Ye come; nor wait your coming nor delay:
Nay fearless, with what scorn
Ye picture China by my brothers torn.

Thy scorn I must accept,
But I'm no coward; pray heed ere more we've wept:
I love Japan so fair,
And China too: this war I cannot bear.

Is there no other way?
Thus do I search my spirit all the day
Nor ever reach a goal;
I live, but only as a phantom soul.

Like Christ who bore our sins upon the cross,
I, too, must bear my country's sins and dross;
Land of my love! Thy sins are grievous to be borne,
My head hangs upon form forlorn.

Ah tears, unbidden tears!
Long separated we.
Alas has come another day
When I must dwell with thee.

Because of his fame and his outstanding leadership, Kagawa's voice was powerful, but it was a lone voice calling in a void. The Japanese military were in command and the war effort was gathering momentum.

Meanwhile affairs in Europe were taking a sinister turn. Austria had been overrun by Hitler, and in October, Czechoslovakia fell. The Munich crisis was upon us.

Had I not been expecting our second child within a few weeks, my husband would have insisted on my leaving Hong Kong. The general feeling was that, if Britain and Germany went to war, Japan would immediately attack Hong Kong. An Empress boat was due to sail the day after the Munich meeting, and finally I prepared to leave within twenty-four hours should the European situation warrant it.

Going down the stairs, I met our German friends from the apartment below. I was startled to see the young wife with her baby in her arms and her husband following with suitcases.

"Are you leaving?" I asked.

"We must," she replied. "The boat is waiting for us."

No more was said, but we soon discovered that a German liner had steamed into port and was evacuating all Germans in the colony. Three days later they were back in the apartment again. The ship had ridden out the crisis at sea. The Munich settlement postponed disaster and the colony settled down.

Our second son, Paul, was born in early November, and we sailed as a family three days before Christmas, 1938. Ships were now calling regularly at Shanghai, which was completely under Japanese control, but we stayed on board and were glad to be at sea again as quickly as possible.

The Pacific crossing was the worst the Empress captain had ever experienced. During the ten days crossing from Yokohama to Vancouver, we were able to be out on deck for only one hour. Finally we arrived in Canada on January 9, 1939, as landed immigrants. Our parents had to stand guarantee for us because, although we had both come to the country as very young children, neither my husband nor I was born in Canada. We were warned that if we were convicted of a crime or became welfare cases, we would be deported. We always wondered what would have happened to us if Dick had been sent to Wales and I to Hong Kong.

Adjusting to life in Canada took time. As Dick remarked, "I went to China with a trunk and a suitcase; I came home with a wife, two children and a van-load of goods."

Coping with a house and two children without the good offices of a cook and an amah was also part of the experience of settling in. I thought of my amah's look of disbelief when I told her I would have to do all the work myself when I went to Canada.

With the approach of spring I began to marvel at the changing seasons, something that we had not experienced during our years in the tropics. I gazed down the boulevard at the trees sprouting their new green leaves and the daffodils nodding along the paths. My throat was tight and tears were close. I hadn't experienced spring for seven years, and the wonder of it overwhelmed me. It seemed to symbolize a new beginning for us all. Dick had decided to give up teaching and enter the business field in Vancouver. We had to find a home to call our own, and we all had to adjust to a new way of life.

David, now almost three, had chattered in Chinese to the amahs, to the boys at my husband's school, and to anyone else he chanced to meet. When we arrived in Canada, however, he sensed this was not the thing to do. My Mother, who spoke fluent Chinese, tried to encourage him to keep up the language, but although he understood her perfectly, he would reply in English. Life was different and he accepted that.

Even as we were busy settling in, our thoughts were in China. We were anxious about what might happen next. The Kuomintang had established itself in West China and continued the war from that base; the Communist forces were holding out in the northwest. An international group of concerned people was successfully running food and medical supplies through the Japanese lines with the help of the Communist Eighth Route Army for the relief of the suffering population in the occupied areas. Men and women trained by Dr. Bethune were carrying on the medical work and Communist tactics were becoming increasingly successful. Through experience, they were learning to organize the people, the government and the army, and to develop programmes to carry out reconstruction. There was in fact a second China which controlled nearly one hundred million people, and the United States sent delegations to confer with this Communist regional government.

There was no let-up in the bitter fighting. The Japanese finally penetrated into the south. Canton had fallen six weeks before we left Hong Kong and we had heard the guns only thirty miles from Hong Kong.

"I'm in the militia reserves now," wrote a friend shortly after we arrived home.

"Must dash off to air-raid precautions training," signed off another friend.

"The women who haven't gone home must take first aid and nursing training," wrote still another. "There aren't many foreign children left in the colony now."

When war broke out in Europe in 1939, Hong Kong was tense, but the Japanese did not attack. The Japanese-Soviet Neutrality Pact signed in April 1941, appeared to remove any danger of Soviet intervention. In China, the conflict between the Kuomintang and the Communists was once more becoming critical. The Communist area of control was expanding and steadily growing more efficient. The increased strength of its armies brought demands for more rights in decision making. The Kuomintang refused, and Chiang sent some of his best troops to blockade the Communists in the northwest.

Because of the war in Europe, China was isolated. The preoccupation of the West and their closing of rail lines and roads to avoid irritating Japan, left China stranded. The only bright spot was the United States' extension of lend-lease to China in 1941.

Then the final blow fell on December 2, 1941, with the invasion of Pearl Harbour. All hell broke loose in the Pacific.

Sidney Ricketts (extreme left) on board S.S. Moldavia, *going through Red Sea, Christmas Day, 1903*

Bridge joining island of Shameen with city of Canton, 1904

Shameen. Office of Shewan Tomes, contractors for first power station in Canton

Curious children watching Sidney Ricketts

Tz'u-hsi, Empress Dowager, power behind the throne, 1861-1908

Sidney Ricketts (standing) and friend after grass hockey game

Sidney Ricketts leaving the new power station, 1905

Sidney Ricketts with construction workers, 1904. Note bamboo scaffolding

Sidney Ricketts (seated) with staff at power house, 1906

Ruth Briscombe and Chinese assistant with class at fifth ward school

Hair styles in imperial China, circa 1908

Briscombe-Ricketts wedding. Canton, October 29, 1908

Author in padded jacket and pants, 1910

Author with parents and nurse-amah, 1910

Detail of group attending reception for Dr. Sun Yat Sen (middle row, second from right) in Canton, May 1912 after his election to Presidency of new Republic. On his right is his secretary, Soong Ai-ling

Chinese church picnic, Vancouver 1913. Sidney Ricketts standing extreme left. In front, Rev. Briscombe (Ruth's father), and second row right Mrs. Briscombe visiting from England 1913. Ruth Ricketts extreme right, third row

Author receiving B.A. from the University of British Columbia, May 1929

Foreign and Chinese staff, St. Hilda's School 1933. Author second row, extreme right

Ricketts-Phillips wedding party and guests at garden reception, December 18, 1934

Entrance to Forbidden City (former imperial palace) where Chairman Mao stood to declare the People's Republic of China, October 1, 1949

Building tractors in a rural community

Workers group during Cultural Revolution studying Marxism and Mao's little red book

Statue of Li Shih Chen (1518-1593), author of 52-volume encyclopedia of Chinese medicine

Studying morse code at Children's Palace, Shanghai

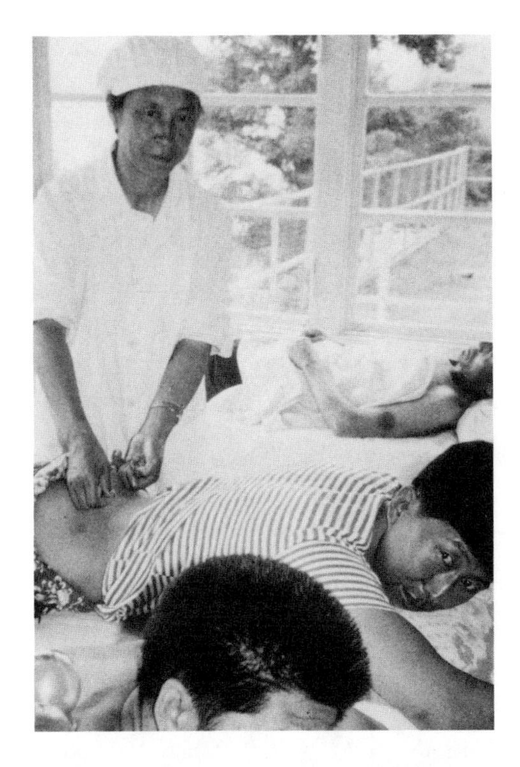

Acupuncture and cupping at a workers' sanatorium in Dairen

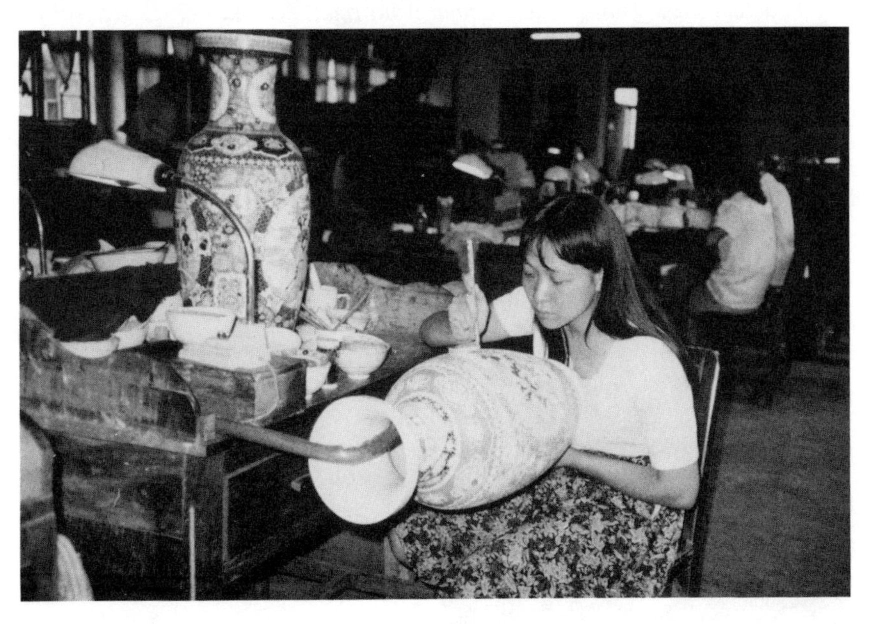

Painting pottery by hand

Women's committee of Chun Gung Metallurgical Powder Products Neighbourhood Factory. Mrs. Han Ji Shun second from right. Newly elected successor on extreme right

103-year-old head of Taoist monastery, Chengdu

The Yangtze Gorges

Buddha at Leshan carved out of mountainside

Author riding a camel on the Mongolian grasslands

Uigher women and children riding a donkey cart on the street in Turfan

14. Japan's Attack and Defeat

When the United States and then Britain declared war on Japan, China joined the western allies and became part of the world-wide conflict. With incredible speed the Japanese offensive rolled on. We were glued to our radios awaiting the fate of Hong Kong. It wasn't long in coming. Japanese troops poured over the hills and on Christmas Day, 1941, Hong Kong fell.

Our friends and fellow workers were interned. News gradually seeped out. St. Stephen's Boys School, after suffering days of atrocities, became an internment camp. An acquaintance who had joined the militia reserves was sent to Japan to work in the mines. One of Dick's fellow workers died from neglect after he was stricken with diphtheria. Others suffered emaciation and broken health from which they never fully recovered. The news literally made us sick.

But in spite of the hardships and horrors, those who eventually came home were able to remember the devotion and care of native Christians in particular. These people, usually at peril of their own lives, did what they could to assist their foreign friends.

"Outside our camp," some friends told us later, "There were some

Christians who periodically slipped eggs over the wall to us. It was dangerous for both those inside and outside. But we had a wonderful man, a Catholic priest, who insisted that he would do the collecting. 'I have no family' he said. 'If I get caught no one else will suffer.'

"There is an amusing side to the story. One day as the priest was gathering the eggs into his little basket, a Japanese guard suddenly appeared. Out of the corner of his eye, the priest saw someone's washing hanging on a line. Nonchalantly, he unpegged some lady's underwear and placed it in the basket, to the bemusement of those prisoners who saw the incident. The unsuspecting guard walked past the innocent-looking basket where the eggs were safely buried under panties and bras."

Some Japanese Christians, trapped by their nation's policy, faced a terrible dilemma.

After the conquest of Soochow, eighty Japanese soldiers attended the University's Christmas service. A few hours later, the order was sent out that all the surrounding villages were to be burned down. Confronted with a problem they could not solve, many of this group refused and then hanged themselves.

In another incident, a group of Chinese women bound in a line were being led to a certain place to be raped. The responsibility for taking them to the destination was given to a Japanese Christian soldier. He set off with them, but upon reaching a church, stopped, and untied their hands. He pointed heavenward, to the church and to himself and then dismissed them.

Money from Christians in Japan was smuggled into China for the relief of Chinese refugees. One Japanese soldier, enjoined by his mother to do all he could to help the Chinese, said in perplexity to his pastor, "How can I do it with a gun in my hand?"

After the war, all our friends corroborated the statement that the most humane internment camps were those run by Japanese officers who had a basic faith rooted in a concern for human life.

After the conquest of the coastal cities, the war became largely based on guerrilla tactics. The Chinese pursued a scorched earth-policy and held on to the vast interior, with the Japanese commanding the cities and key communication centres. The new capital of China was Chungking, where the national government functioned. With the opening of the Burma Road, communications with the outside world were resumed.

The building of the Burma Road was a prodigious feat. In the book *McLure, The China Years* by Munroe Scott, Dr. Bob McLure tells of his hair-raising journey over the road during the early days of the war.

> The Burma Road was still officially secret. It would become known as the greatest military road ever built. Begun secretly in 1937, hundreds of thousands of men, women and children had been "recruited" from many areas in China, and sent into the western mountains to claw a highway through and over those same mountains into the British territory of Burma . . .
>
> The task was being carried out without western implements, in other words with hoe, hammer, pick, shovel, baskets and bare hands. Now, however, that road and the rail line from Indo-China were the only supply routes into Free China. The Japanese had closed the Yangtze River to all shipping, and the British were retaliating by preparing to let war munitions and anything else, flow through Burma into China . . .
>
> The road spiralled snakelike through mountain passes,it clung leechlike to the sides of towering precipices, it hung stringlike across canyons so deep their bottoms were lost in darkness. Vehicles climbed to 8,000 feet and then almost plunged to 2,500 feet where a steel suspension bridge thrust across the Salween River gorge. On the fifth day the road led into even more tortuous conditions and to even more dizzying heights. Hill gradients increased to fifteen percent and more. The road itself climbed to 9,500 feet of elevation.

Coolies, brought as forced labour from Honan province, reported that 20,000 men and women from their area had been building the road, but malaria, dysentery, accidents and heavy work had reduced their number to 100. Some were wise enough to resist the unrelenting pressure. A western coordinator, coming across a coolie sitting by the roadside with his load resting beside him, asked the reason for the delay.

"I'm just waiting for my soul to catch up with my body," replied the unhurried man.

An inscription in bold characters on a towering cliff proclaimed: "This road was built by the natives of this district without the aid of foreign implements." It was part of the price China was paying for the anti-Japanese war.

As the war progressed, the Americans became closely associated with Chiang Kai-shek. Impressed with the discipline and initiative of the Communists, the United States urged Chiang to cooperate with the Communists and establish a coalition government, but Chiang steadfastly refused.

Meanwhile, from his headquarters in Yenan, Mao was building a second China, a new social and political entity which attracted foreign delegations. Controlling over one hundred million people, with one million party members and an army of over one million, Mao was able to gain experience in government and lay the foundations for the future.

As Japan relentlessly pursued her conquests in the Pacific, the Chinese resistance gained new respect in the United States. Moreover, China was tying down half the Japanese army and costing Japan billions of dollars. But the cost of the war to China was enormous. She had lost revenue from ports on the coast occupied by Japan; she was crippled by military expenditures. To pay for the war, the government had issued more money which resulted in runaway inflation. The business class was almost destroyed, and over three million casualties had been sustained in the fighting. The people were weary after eight years of civil war and resistance to Japan.

With the fall of Japan in 1945, China emerged as a victor. She now had an honourable place in the world and replaced Japan as the chief Asiatic power. Chiang's position seemed assured. But the sudden collapse of Japan after the dropping of the atomic bombs created a problem for the Kuomintang. It was necessary for the government army to reach the Japanese- and Soviet-occupied territories to receive the Japanese surrender and gather in the enemy arms and supplies. But the large, disciplined Communist army, closer to the areas in question, launched an offensive in the closing days of the war and ordered the Japanese to surrender to them. With the help of the Americans, however, Chiang's troops were airlifted to the scene and temporarily gained the upper hand.

Convinced that the United States would never permit a Communist victory, Chiang pursued a policy of noncooperation with his political foes, but under pressure from the United States, he finally agreed to a conference with Mao Tse-tung in Chungking. Mao, confident of his ultimate success, appeared conciliatory and reasonable, but after six weeks of negotiations, little was accomplished. Civil war loomed again.

General Marshall was sent by Washington to attempt unification and reconciliation. Under his guidance, another conference was held which set up a system of government with Kuomintang (KMT), Communist (CCP), and Democratic League representatives. In addition, agreement was reached on the integration of the KMT and CCP armies. However, neither of the two main factions really trusted each other. Only Marshall's presence kept the peace.

Encouraged by the apparent success of negotiations, Chiang disregarded agreements and unilaterally called a National Assembly, which the Communists and Democratic League boycotted. Civil war erupted. A bitterly disappointed Marshall left China. For a time Chiang's army achieved success, but in September, 1947 the tide turned. To cover the conquered areas, Chiang had to assign large numbers of troops to garrison duty while the Communists had meanwhile been training and expanding. An ill-advised government campaign in Manchuria in 1948 cost Chiang nearly half a million of his best troops. At this point the Communists moved in to attack, and Chiang's demoralized army lost two divisions to defection as well as to severe defeats.

The Communist juggernaut rolled on. Between September 1948 and January 1949, Chiang had lost a million and a half men. On April 21, 1949, Mao's troops crossed the Yangtze. With the imminent conquest of South China, Mao, on October 1, 1949, proclaimed the People's Republic of China from the steps of the Forbidden City, the ancient Imperial Palace of Peking.

"We call it 'Liberation'," the Chinese told us when we visited the country in the 1970s. "Since Liberation" was on the tip of every tongue when people told us their life story.

Probably the best commentary on the meaning of Liberation was given me by a farm woman. "Until I was twenty-five," she said, "life dragged on, and every morning I dreaded to see the run rise. Then came Liberation. Daylight came to mean more than backbreaking, unending work. I had no education and couldn't even recognize my own name, but in 1952 literacy classes were organized and I began to study. In 1958, I was formally declared literate, no longer an 'open-eyed blind person,' as adults were called who could not read. Now I'm assistant director of my twelve-hundred-member commune."

For people who had aspirations for an education, the word "Liberation" had special meaning. Mr. and Mrs. Wang, a retired couple now living in a four-room house in the city of Tsingtao, told me their story. Their present living room — furnished with velour chesterfield, armchairs, bookcase, tape recorder, television and coffee table — contrasted dramatically with their life before Liberation.

"I was born in 1918," Mr. Wang began. "Although my parents were farmers, they were able to give me a little education. A small private school in my village charged one string of cash per year." Cash were small coins worth less than a cent, with a hole in the middle so that they could be tied together on a string.

For a time the boy — an only son — was able to learn the rudiments of reading and writing. But times were hard. In 1932, his father went to Dalian in north-east China to get work in a factory run by the Japanese. He decided to take his son with him. The father was determined that the boy should have an education and somehow he managed to pay for primary school. But when war broke out between China and Japan, life was so difficult that in 1942, father and son returned to their home town. The Japanese, the Kuomintang and the Communists were all occupying parts of their province, but the father sent his son to a dormitory school fifty kilometres from their home so that he would not be drafted into the Kuomintang army.

"I don't know how my father managed it," admitted Mr. Wang.

By 1943, part of Shandong was liberated by the Communists, and Mr. Wang began to work for the People's Government. After the Japanese surrender in 1946, most of the province came under the People's Government and Mr. Wang became a school teacher. He had had only one year of high school education, but teachers were badly needed and few were qualified. Conditions were very bad. There were no supplies. Children brought their own stools; their desks were made of earth. Parents were not very supportive because they wanted the children at home to help. Mr. Wang, however, persevered and gradually improved his own education. With the proclamation of the People's Republic in 1949, education became a priority.

At this time Mr. Wang met his wife. She was an only daughter and had had some education, so together they taught school. At the same time, they raised a family of five sons and two daughters, all of whom finished high school. One completed university and is now teaching marine studies. Mr. Wang retired at the age of sixty-four and enjoyed many activities and remained devoted to helping his eleven grandchildren. It was a happy ending to a life of poverty and struggle in chaotic times.

15. Chengdu Experiences Liberation

After 1949, the West's fear of Communism and the closing of China's doors made it very difficult to obtain unbiased reports and to assess developments. There were foreigners in the country for some time after Liberation, however, and they did provide information frequently ignored by the media and by Western governments.

Professor Earl Willmott and his wife Katharine remained in China on staff at West China Union University, from 1949 to 1952. Their first-hand experience of life in China during those early years of Liberation is very revealing. Mrs. Willmott described events to me as they happened in the city of Chengdu.

First of all, there were the rumours. Servants would come running to the foreigners with tales told in the market place. "Have you heard," they would say, "that when the Communists come they are going to throw anyone who has been helping a Westerner into jail?" Teachers came in distress. "Have you heard that when the Communists come they are going to take every teacher and marry her to a peasant to make things more equal?" The rumours were endless.

Even the University Senate was busily devising service projects in order to avoid any of the dire predictions about the fate of intellectuals. As the Communist armies came closer and closer to the city, which was some thousand miles from Peking, the atmosphere became charged with apprehension.

Chiang Kai-shek and the remnants of his army made their last stand near Chengdu. But just before Christmas 1949, Chiang and his entourage took flight to Taiwan. As a result, there was no great battle for the city. A few shots were heard in the vicinity of a temple outside the city, followed by an ominous calm. On Christmas morning, a runner interrupted the university church service with the announcement that the Kuomintang troops had all turned themselves over to the People's Liberation Army. All China was now in the hands of the Communists.

"We weren't frightened," Mrs. Willmott assured me, "but naturally we wondered what the outcome would be. We stood for over two hours on the balcony of a friend's store at the chief crossroad and watched the victory parade go through the streets of the city."

It was an orderly, friendly procession. First came trucks of waving, shouting students and other progressives who, until that morning, had been the secret underground. They were, no doubt, augmented by some people anxious to show how much they were on the bandwagon. Then came truck after truck, mostly captured American vehicles, loaded with Kuomintang turn-coats, many with hastily-pasted red stars on their Kuomintang caps. And finally, swinging along among gun carriages, jeeps and pack animals, came the PLA (People's Liberation Army). They had no snappy uniforms and affected no goose-stepping, but clad in their combat padded winter garments, they strode along on the last long mile to Liberation.

The population received them very well because the army turned out to be people like themselves — peasants and workers. Here and there a soldier would step out and talk with a group in the crowd, joking with them, telling them tales of the march and explaining in the simplest words the significance of what was happening. Once in a while, a few of them would break ranks and do a peasant dance or teach the bystanders a Liberation song. Soon there was a gay holiday spirit, and people began to sing and dance with them. Any sense of apprehension melted away.

Policemen, who usually held a truncheon to whack the heads of careless rickshaw pullers, were holding bright red megaphones and shouting "Careful there, little brother. Don't get under the feet of the horses," or "Stand back a little, comrade, so your neighbours can see too."

After the excitement of the parade and the arrival of the PLA, great changes began to take place, not with bullets but with talk. In 1950 people were talking all over China: six hundred million people talking. They were talking in small groups of fifteen to twenty in every institution, every bank, every place of business, every school and university, every block of every street, and every district of every countryside in China. They spoke of something called The New Democracy, something calling for a complete change from their former ideas, ideals and ways of living. There was no more talk of idealistic abstractions such as liberty, equality, fraternity, faith, hope or charity. There was just one ethic promoted for the new society: the good of all the people. This phrase was heard in all discussion; everything was measured by it — everything in their institutions, in their city, in their country and in the world.

"We Westerners were measured by it too," added Mrs. Willmott. "Our capitalistic philosophy, our 'rugged individualism,' our self-centred ambitions for getting ahead and for money and power were judged in the light of this new philosophy. You can imagine how we began to take a more penetrating look at our own culture."

Mrs. Willmott belonged to a group of teachers and representative students in the English department. They faced many questions: how could English courses contribute to the good of the people, what courses contributed most to the good of the people, what courses were useless and what courses could be useful and to whom.

There was a great deal of criticism of teachers and institutions, but teachers were not the only ones faulted. Students came in for their share too. Dull, dogmatic teachers were certainly criticized, but interesting teachers who had rapport with their students were held up as examples and asked to demonstrate their teaching methods to others. Students were criticized for "playboy attitudes" or for aspirations to a place in society several notches higher than others.

The criticism was effective, Mrs. Willmott assured me. It changed attitudes, and a new honesty pervaded the campus. Numerous teachers confessed to abusing privileges or using or taking university property for their own use, or to placing their own interests before those of the people. Cheating in exams, which had been widespread in the past, was now held to be against the people's good. By 1952, when the Willmotts left Chengdu, the whole university was on the honour system.

Even in sports the attitude was different. In basketball games, the losing team, after congratulating the victors, sat down with them and asked them to explain the plays that won them the victory. The motto in sports became "Friendship first, competition second."

Education was undoubtedly a key to change, but since ninety percent of the Chinese people were engaged in agriculture and were largely illiterate, basic transformation had to be in that area.

Mrs. Willmott spoke of the thrill of seeing the peasants each receive their little plots of land, of watching as the small red paper flags were placed at the corner of each little one-third acre plot. Then followed the family celebration dinners in the mud courtyards, several ounces of pork added to the usual rice and pickles. Later these peasants met on the university campus grounds in cooperative planning groups, to discuss agricultural affairs in their district, their chairman standing up half abashed in unaccustomed dignity.

I mentioned to Mrs. Willmott that we had heard horror tales of widespread retaliation against landlords.

"Yes," she agreed. "We saw a mass trial of a landlord on our campus."

She described the kneeling, cringing landlord, already convicted of murder and rape by an investigating committee of cadres and tenants. The shouting, accusing peasants were gathered there to learn that they were really free, and they saw the landlord led away to have the fateful sentence carried out. There were executions, a natural result of centuries of oppression and exploitation. The national leaders did call for re-education of the landowners rather than their deaths. But it was hard in such a vast country, with the turmoil of change and the bitterness of the past, to control local actions.

With the illiteracy rate so high, the authorities had to find ways to put over their ideas to the people. There were discussion groups everywhere, and movements such as the San Fan, or Three Anti-movement, which stressed antiwaste, anti-corruption and anti-bureaucracy or anti-self promotion. People discussed how they had been infected by the old ideas and ways, and how they could reform their thinking. Mao's simple sayings were taught and broadcast to explain the direction and meaning of the new society. Loud speakers were mounted on street corners, in railway cars and buses — everywhere people congregated. Until adult education classes were established and universal education was a reality, mass education had to begin with the wide-spread spoken word.

As I mulled over Mrs. Willmott's comments I was reminded of a well-known Chinese tale which I first read in *We the Chinese*, edited by Deidre and Neale Hunter. Mao used the story to great advantage in his writings penned in 1945 just before the close of World War II. The task ahead for the Communists looked formidable indeed, but the story said it all:

> There is an ancient Chinese fable called "The Foolish Old Man Who Removed the Mountain." It tells of an old man who lived in northern China long, long ago and was known as the Foolish Old Man of North Mountain. His house faced south and beyond his doorway stood two great peaks, Taihang and Wangru, obstructing his way. The Old Man called his sons, and, hoe in hand, they began with great determination to dig up those mountains. Another greybeard, known as the Wise Old Man, saw them and said derisively, "How silly of you to do this! It is quite impossible for you few to dig up those two huge mountains.
>
> "The Foolish Old Man replied, "When I die my sons will carry on; when they die there will be my grandsons and then their sons and grandsons, and so on to infinity. High as they are, the mountains cannot grow any higher, and with every bit we dig they will be that much lower. Why can't we clear them away?"
>
> Having refuted the Wise Old Man's wrong view, he went on digging every day, unshaken in his conviction. God was moved by this and He sent down two angels who carried the mountains away on their backs.
>
> Today two big mountains lie like a dead weight on the Chinese people. One is imperialism; the other is feudalism. The Chinese Communist Party has long made up its mind to dig them up. We must persevere and work unceasingly and we too will touch God's heart. Our God is none other than the masses of the Chinese people. If they stand up and dig together with us, why can't those two mountains be cleared away?"

16. Opening the Bamboo Curtain

In the spirit of "The Foolish Old Man," the Communists began to tackle the enormous task of revitalizing, re-educating and reforming their country. The door began to close on the outside world. If the "twin mountains of imperialism and feudalism" were to be moved, no one could do it but the Chinese themselves. Our friends who had remained in China were asked to leave, and the "bamboo curtain" was lowered.

As our family life became more demanding and contact with China became difficult, there was a lull in our China interests. In 1947, we added twins — a girl, Ruth, and a boy, Rhys — to our family. With four growing children at different stages of development, life was far from dull.

After World War II, Dick and I helped to organize a Cooperative Rural Community on 130 acres near Nanaimo, on central Vancouver Island. A group of us established a community where each worked at his or her own profession or trade, but shared with each other. Numerous demobilized soldiers wished to join us, but the government refused to allow them to put their demob pay into a co-op. Times were good and jobs available, but housing was non-existent in the area around the co-op. Finally, after three years we had to disband, terminating an interesting and enriching experiment.

Dick was able to secure work as an accountant at St. Joseph's Hospital in Victoria. We were offered a nine-acre property on the outskirts of the city and we all enjoyed the space and the opportunity to raise goats and chickens and have an extensive garden. Our well dried up however, forcing us to move, and for ten years we were happy with a two-acre property easily accessible to the city. These were happy, busy years as we became involved in the life of the community and in our children's activities.

St. Joseph's at this time was accepting on their service staff many displaced persons from Europe. Dick became their spokesman through the hospital workers union. This led him into the Church Labour Council and into some political activity.

With the children at various levels of schooling, we, as parents, became involved. Dick was active in parent-teacher organizations while my activities lay chiefly in politics, church and the youth groups in which our children were involved.

In 1956, I decided to return to teaching. All four children were in school and the two older boys ready for university. Family demands were heavy. I was fortunate to be accepted in a senior high school near at hand and remained with the Saanich School District, on the outskirts of Victoria, for nineteen years.

During the late fifties and early sixties youth was on the move. Student tours to Europe were common. As my interest lay in the Orient however, I conceived the idea in 1960 of a tour to Asia. Gathering together a few leaders, we laid plans, speaking largely to church youth groups. We talked ambitiously of chartering a 140-passenger plane, but in the end settled for a regular flight with a group of sixty-seven, forty of whom were under twenty-years of age. China was still inaccessible, but in 1962, we spent nearly two months travelling outbound by ship and returning by plane, with three weeks in Japan, a week in Korea, three weeks in Hong Kong, and for some a side trip to Thailand.

The only glimpse we had of China was over the barbed-wire demarcation line in the New Territories outside Hong Kong. Our older boys were now studying and working on their own, but the twins accompanied me. Two years later, they also went with me on another organized tour to Europe, covering the western countries as well as Poland, Czechoslovakia and Russia.

I was still waiting for the opportunity to get to China. A small crack opened in 1965, when the Chinese permitted the Canada-China Friendship Association to take a group to China. But with the outbreak of the Cultural Revolution in 1966, contacts were again broken.

In 1969, the principal of my school approached me about the possibility of a student tour to Japan for Expo '70. The school board was enthusiastic and the idea became so popular that I ended up with a group of 180 students between the ages of twelve and eighteen, and twenty adults. We spent a week at Expo, a week in Korea and a week in Tokyo, managing it all on $600 per person, including the special charter fare of $300. It was on this trip that I was inspired to think further.

"When are you going to take us to China?" asked one of my former students. In answer to that I began applying for permission. In 1972, I got a nibble from China. How many people would I be bringing, and what were their names and ages? As I had had no intimation that China would consider receiving a group, I had not organized a tour and was unprepared for such a question. When I explained this in my reply, I heard nothing further. But I kept on applying.

Finally on Christmas Eve, 1973, a terse letter arrived: "You may bring twenty-five people to China entering June 7, exiting June 22, 1974." My face fell. I had told China that the dates must be in the summer because of school holidays. Then I began to dream. Perhaps the school board would allow me three week's leave and even permit other teachers and some students to join me. The Saanich Teachers' Association agreed to lend its name as sponsor, and I approached the board. Permission was kindly granted and several teachers and senior students took advantage of the opportunity. The remainder of the places were filled with eager, interested persons in the community.

Excitement was intense. Going to China was still a misty dream for most people. We didn't know what to expect or what was in store for us, but off we went with keen anticipation. After landing by plane in Hong Kong, we took the train to Canton, disembarking part way at the border town of Sumchun. There, bursting with curiosity, we crossed the bridge into China. From this point on, we were accompanied on the train and throughout our tour by Mr. Li, an excellent English-speaking guide. He sat down beside me on the train, introduced me to Mrs. Chen, our second guide, and then said, "What do you want to see?"

I hadn't anticipated having any choice, but quickly thought of everything I could in the five cities we were to visit, consulting with some of the other knowledgeable members of the tour. The list seemed impossibly long. The following morning, however, I was told that all the arrangements we had requested had been confirmed. Looking over the schedule, I found that we were to see all we had asked for and more besides.

As the train sped along I thought of the many times I had ridden this line: in 1910, sitting on my mother's knee or more likely nestled in the arms of a doting nurse-amah; in the 1930s when I was teaching in Canton and making frequent trips to Hong Kong to visit Dick; and now June 7, 1974, entering for the first time the People's Republic of China. What changes would I see? How would the new China look?

I wondered how China had been able to cope with the enormous problems she had faced in 1949. For one thing, inflation at that time had reached ridiculous proportions. A letter, which in 1947 had cost one Chinese dollar to mail, by 1949 cost eighty-two million. Million dollar bills were common currency. No one attempted to save money as it was soon worthless.

One of my friends, returning with a group of missionaries, submitted a bill to the Church Board for their dinner on arrival in San Francisco. A startled accountant questioned the several million-dollar cost of the meal. My friend, used to dealing in millions, had forgotten to put the decimal in the right place.

The first task of the new government in 1949 had been to issue a new currency and ban all foreign mediums of exchange. Workers' wages were tied to the basic prices of rice, flour, coal, oil and cotton cloth. By the end of 1950, the economic situation had been stabilized and the government budget balanced.

Little news had come out of China in those twenty-five years since Liberation. Now I was visiting China and was able to ask questions. Peasants readily agreed that there had been violence, but explained that it varied considerably.

The property which was consolidated into communes had originally belonged to several wealthy landlords or rich peasants. When the government took over all the land, some of the landowners, seeing the writing on the wall, grudgingly agreed to cooperate with the poor peasants. Many did not however, and "accusation meetings" were commonly held when centuries of bitterness welled up. In some cases, revengeful peasants took matters into their own hands. After brief public trials, the accused were often summarily shot. Unfortunately, the landlord's children suffered severe discrimination, often for many years.

By the end of 1952, the agrarian revolution was completed. Three hundred million peasants, most of whom had previously eked out an existence on rented land or as hired labourers, were now landowners. The individual plots were small nevertheless, and it soon became obvious that individuals working their own tiny field could never produce enough food for the developing nation. The drive began, step by step, towards collective ownership. Every district struggled with the pros and cons of these new ideas. First, farmers were encouraged to work together in mutual aid teams. Then came cooperatives and, finally, the large communes. Families remained on their land in their villages, but the whole area produced a unified plan. It was a completely new way of life, but it made diking, water conservation, irrigation, electrification and crop experimentation possible. Production soared.

One of the first visits our group made after arriving in Canton in June, 1974, was to a 56,000-member commune producing fruit, vegetables, rice and sugar cane. As was the custom on all our visits, there was a "tea briefing," when the manager, after a little preamble lauding the new system, gave us a run down of facts and figures.

"This is one of 229 production teams in our commune," he stated. "We are responsible to the next level, the brigade, and it in turn is responsible to the commune where the overall plan originates. Besides our agricultural products we also have fish ponds and a little animal husbandry. Small factories help to make us more self-sufficient. When the women are not needed in the fields they make extra for the community by producing machine-made garments or assembling and repairing tractors."

After this introduction, he took us out to see their water conservation program which had quadrupled production. Then he showed us the clinic. "Before Liberation," he said, "there were only three private clinics and three doctors in this whole area, and these facilities were just for the wealthy. Now each team has a clinic, the commune has a hospital, and there are 360 medical personnel including the 'barefoot doctors' (paramedics) and the dentists. Services are free."

The primary school nearby was simple but full of busy young students. The wooden desks were plain and very well worn; the rooms somewhat dingy. The classes were very orderly however, and the children were occupied with books and scribblers. They leapt to their feet when we arrived, and, after showing us their work, gave a short programme of songs and recitations.

As we walked on, I was surprised to see an outdoor sports arena with electric lighting for evening games. A few young men in their mid-morning break were throwing basketballs.

"We're proud of our little stadium," commented our guide. "We needed somewhere for our young people to play, where they could have friendly games with other communes or factory teams from the city. We decided to build a basketball court and seats for the spectators. We made the bricks ourselves. Everyone was asked to help in the evening after work. When we had enough bricks made, people came to build the stadium. Because we had electricity in our commune, we put up lights for the playing field. Tonight our team is hosting a team from the tractor factory in the next town."

Our guide drove us along the country roads leading through the huge commune with its village production teams, each responsible for rice growing, orchard cultivation or vegetable horticulture. I recognized the small villages that had been there, doubtless when my mother had visited the countryside, and were certainly there when I lived in Canton. But the villages were different. Gone were the torpor of poverty, the flies and the sick children. During the entire trip in 1974, we saw only two flies which brought from us exclamations of dismay. We had come to accept the fact that the command to "Swat Flies" had been carried out to an incredible conclusion.

One experience in that summer of 1974 stands out clearly in my mind — largely, I suppose, because it typified the change I saw all around me. We were standing on the beautiful new Nanking Bridge, which in itself was a tribute to the unbeatable determination of the local people. I pointed to an attractive block of apartments fronting a small park.

"What are those buildings?" I inquired.

"The homes of the bridge maintenance crew and some factory workers," I was told.

As I gazed at them, I thought of the pitiable workers who had lived in makeshift huts or in the open under the old bridges, their feet wrapped in rags and their bodies barely covered with flimsy garments. True, they probably now shared a kitchen and a bathroom, and the rooms would be small. But at least they were warm and dry, with food to eat, clothes to wear, medical attention and most of all, rights and privileges.

Obviously life had changed and I was eager to discover the extent and depth of that change. China in June of 1974, was still suffering under the Cultural Revolution. Everything we were told was prefaced by the standard opening remarks referring to the poverty and exploitation of the past and the great reforms brought about by the Party and Chairman Mao. We listened to the children singing "I am a sunflower and Chairman Mao is the sun" and the old folks praising the Party because they could now retire knowing they would be cared for. But underneath all the propaganda was indisputable evidence of vast improvements. I kept saying to my group, "You hear the songs and listen to the words, but I see the changes. I simply can't believe what they have done in twenty-five years."

When I returned to Canada people said to me, "Are there really no more slums in China?"

"It depends on what you call slums," I replied. "The filthy hovels of destitution are gone. Some have been repaired until the occupants can be moved into new apartments that are being built as fast as construction materials can be produced. The emaciated, sore-covered children have disappeared. Visitors comment on the healthy-looking youngsters who win the hearts of the foreigners. Everyone has food, clothes and a place to live. Given time, the transformation will be more startling."

And I was to see some of that startling transformation on my visits from 1980 to 1989.

17. The Cultural Revolution

On my return from the 1974 trip to China, there was a great demand for me to speak to groups. Not everyone was entirely sympathetic, but interest was keen. One of the most common questions was: "When are you going again?"

I considered this question and decided that if it were possible I would try for another tour in 1976. I retired from teaching in June 1975, after nineteen years of involvement in English, history, drama, typing and shorthand, and eventually as school librarian. But retirement meant only leaving the classroom for other activities. I was appointed to the Board of Governors of the University of Victoria and to the Advisory Planning Commission of the Saanich Municipality. Both of these positions brought wider and more interesting community involvement. Church work and politics rounded out busy days and weeks.

As interest in China was widespread, I embarked on a province-wide speaking tour accompanied by a couple who had been to China with me. We showed slides and described our experiences. I was also interviewed on several radio programs. It was evident that there was support for another tour. Finally I received permission in late 1975 to bring a group the following summer.

Arriving in Beijing (as Peking was now called) on July 27, 1976, we had a rather frightening beginning. A few hours after we deplaned,

Beijing was shaken by the massive Tangshan earthquake, in which a quarter of a million people at least were killed. As we were only about one hundred miles away, we experienced severe shocks. We were shaken out of bed at 3:40 a.m. and, making our way through unlighted, plaster-strewn halls, joined the populace of the city on the streets. Later in the day, another quake made our hotel uninhabitable, so we spent the night under the gracious care of the Canadian embassy staff at their headquarters. The following day we were sent to North China and missed seeing Beijing entirely.

The dreadful task of coping with the catastrophe taxed national resources. Railway stations were piled high with supplies for Tangshan and airplanes were redirected to the area. The Gang of Four, then in control of the government, allowed little news to be broadcast overseas and refused international aid. I have found that many people were unaware of one of the world's greatest earthquake tragedies. Practically the whole city of Tangshan was levelled. Entire families were wiped out. One of my guides a few years later told me that she was an orphan. Living in Beijing at the time, she was unhurt, but her mother, father and two sisters in Tangshan were killed. Ten thousand miners, trapped underground, were nearly all miraculously brought up safely through ventilators and partially damaged shafts, only to reach home and find their families all dead.

The change of itinerary did give us an opportunity to see the industrial development in such northern centres as the big steel producing city of Anshan, the industrial city of Shenyang, and the busy port of Dalian.

As the tour progressed, we tried to assess some of the impact of the Cultural Revolution which had been in progress for ten years. Rather sinister reports had been coming out of China about the power of the ultra-leftists, commonly known as the Gang of Four which included Mao's wife Chiang Ch'ing. There were accounts of violence and of great suffering caused by the upheaval when intellectuals were disgraced, imprisoned or sent to the country to work on farms. Theory was scoffed at; examinations were dispensed with. Uneducated peasants and army personnel were raised to high educational positions, under the basic premise that wisdom lay with the common people. Standards naturally fell however, and the educational system was eventually in a state of collapse.

It was difficult to discover the true nature of the Cultural Revolution. Outwardly, some of the results seemed favourable. We felt that the fact that all students had to serve two years on a farm or in a factory before proceeding to higher education was a good idea, particularly in a country where manual labour had always been considered degrading. But we later discovered that two years often lengthened to four or six years, and for some, it became permanent banishment to the countryside. Nor were the farmers keen on integrating thousands of raw city youngsters each year into their agricultural programme.

The Cultural Revolution had begun in late 1965 as an offensive against the literary community which Mao felt was not supportive enough of his Revolution. He insisted that literature and art should be part of the Revolutionary struggle. Articles and counter articles appeared in the press and literary journals until it became apparent that the Cultural Revolution was not just an effort to make the literary and artistic world subservient to the Revolution. It was now obvious that it was a call to the masses to criticize and destroy all the elements within the nation that might be considered counter-revolutionary. Those who had responded to an earlier call by Mao to "let a thousand flowers blossom" found that those very "flowers" were their downfall. Anyone who had expressed ideas that deviated from the accepted line was in danger. In this way Mao found an opportunity to get rid of those who were not prepared to accept the Revolution unconditionally, and were therefore considered revisionists.

A call had gone out to the masses. Big character posters, in which anyone could criticize anyone in a position of authority, became popular. Meetings proliferated. Debate and discussion were endless, in an effort to combat "revisionism" and "capitalist roadism."

Universities and schools were in turmoil. Theoretical courses were attacked by the politically-oriented students. Teaching methods and curriculum were condemned as impractical and "not serving the people." Bitter arguments arose about the respective importance of theoretical learning and manual labour, between city and country and between peasants and intellectuals. Teachers and students were involved in endless discussions on the relationship between education and politics. All schools and universities became subject to investigation and most were eventually closed.

Criticism spread from the educational system to every city and town. Party members and bureaucrats became the targets. Anyone deemed to have strayed from the "revolutionary way" came under attack. Work teams were organized to search out those who were considered enemies of the new regime, or, on the other hand, those who had simply acquired bad habits and could be re-educated. False accusations and persecution became rampant. Student bodies and factory workers met to evaluate and criticize their teachers and workmates.

I found a very graphic example in the work force. At the time of Liberation the state had taken over all industry, but obviously had no ready-made managerial staff to place in command. Managers willing to cooperate with the new regime were appointed to positions of authority so that there would not be a complete breakdown in industry. Gradually the workers assumed more responsibility for decisions, electing from their ranks the cadres or management personnel who ran and organized production. As the Cultural Revolution developed, the former experts who advised and helped manage the industries became suspect.

A friend told me of her family's experience at the time. "My father was an exporter of tea," she explained. "After Liberation he was asked to carry on the business as before. He gradually turned over his capital to the government in return for the position of vice-manager. He was permitted to retain his family home and we children received our education in the state schools and universities. But when the Cultural Revolution came, my father was denounced as a bourgeois right-roader, fired from his job, stripped of his rights and his home, and left with twenty-four yuan a month for living expenses.

"By this time I was a professor, married to another professor, and I had to give support to my mother and father. Then as the Cultural Revolution became more fanatical, all intellectuals were suspect. My husband, my father and I were sent to the countryside to work in the fields, and my mother was left stranded. Perhaps because I was young, I was less severely treated than the older professors, and after several years, my husband and I were permitted to resume teaching. Eventually my father was appointed janitor in his old company."

After the Gang of Four were arrested and condemned, a happier ending was added to the story. The father was reinstated, and the home, which had been made into apartments, was returned to the family. The father was retired on a pension but still used his expertise to advise the state in the field of imports and exports.

While educated families like these were suffering the indignities of this upheaval, student groups, known as Red Guards, fanned out across the country to call on the people to cleanse their society of bureaucrats and opponents of the Revolution and to destroy everything that smacked of superstition and old ideas. The opposition to the "four olds" (old ideas, old culture, old habits and old customs) unfortunately led to destruction of priceless works of art and ancient books.

Mao felt that the disturbance resulting from all this confrontation was worth the risk. By 1966, a whole generation had grown up who had not personally experienced the revolutionary struggle. He therefore encouraged the debate and criticism that led to revolutionary action.

"Why did you let the Cultural Revolution happen?" I asked one professor.

"There were two reasons," she explained. "In the first place the Party had done so much for us that we trusted their judgement. And secondly, the Chinese people have not yet overcome their unquestioning obedience to the dictates of rulers. But," she added, "one good effect is that it has taught us to think for ourselves."

The direction of the Revolution was not totally unopposed. Acts of violence were condemned and opposition to the Red Guards was organized. But Mao was very much in control and used the Revolution to consolidate his position and destroy opposition. It was a move calculated to create a delicate balance between central authority and local revolutionary activity. As a result, the principle of democratic centralism emerged.

By the time I visited China in 1974 and 1976, revolutionary committees had been set up to manage every aspect of life. Every institution was run by a revolutionary committee chosen by the workers, be it factory, commune, school or business. Whenever we visited an institution the opening sentence was always: "This is Mr. (or Mrs.) — , Chairperson of the Revolutionary Committee of — (the particular place we were visiting)."

We soon came to understand that this chairperson was a manager elected by the workers. The committee that made decisions and ran the organization was also chosen by the commune, factory, business workers or students and teachers.

We felt there was merit in this plan of worker self-management. But the lack of managerial skills and particularly, the priority given to party affiliation and political purity, tended often to detract from the success of the operation.

Introductions at the places we visited were stereotyped. After Mr. Chang introduced himself as the vice-president of the Revolutionary Committee of the Hsin Chiao Agricultural Commune, he gave current figures of production and some history of the endeavour. His closing remarks followed a pattern: "Living standards have improved. Before Liberation, people lived a miserable life because of feudalism, imperialism and bureaucratic capitalism, with not enough to eat and wear. Now we have many new buildings and new houses and every family has electricity, a radio and bicycles. Forty-five catties of rice are allocated to every person, including each child. There is vigorous development under the leadership of Chairman Mao, and the divorce of anyone from manual labour and political struggle has been wiped out." By the time we had finished our visits we almost felt we could recite the introduction by heart.

When I arrived for my second visit in 1976, violent disturbances had petered out and life seemed to be running on an even keel. But it was hard to assess the mood of the people. The briefings we were given as we visited factories and farms, schools and hospitals, indicated tremendous progress, but the strong doses of propaganda and impressive statistics were somewhat overdone. There was no doubt, however, that great strides had been and were being made in the lives of one quarter of the world's population.

We found that everyone had to belong to a study group. We were shown classes of workers sitting in a circle during their lunch hour or after work, as they studied Mao's little red book or the works of Lenin, Engels and Marx.

Jack Chen, an internationally recognized journalist, describes in his excellent book, *A Year in Upper Felicity*, his life in a Chinese village during the Cultural Revolution when he was sent down to live with the peasants. He recalls all the discussion that went on over the new constitution drafted in the National Congress, and describes the depth of the arguments as he and the peasant farmers sat in a ditch out of the direct sun during a tea break. Millions of people everywhere were tuning in to their new evolving society.

The children, too, were all part of this educational process. We heard little ones in kindergarten lustily chanting "Serve the People," "Love Labour and Work Hard," and "We Have Friends All Over the World." All through the school system we saw and heard dances, songs and plays lauding honesty, courage, patriotism and friendship, both with the minority peoples within their own borders and with people around the world. In one school we saw a table-tennis dance group of five girls and five boys with ping-pong bats in one hand and flowers in the other, sing about the tiny little ball representing friendship to all the people of the world. Again we heard the emphasis on the national sports slogan, Friendship First, Competition Second.

This melding of entertainment and moral and political teaching was also evident in adult presentations. In 1974 and 1976, we were taken to see revolutionary opera which was all that was permitted in that genre. It was colourful and exciting and gave an interesting picture of the new ideas. The opera *The Taking of Tiger Mountain by Strategy*, depicted a famous manoeuvre which succeeded in ridding a district of its hated gangsters. It was spectacular. The acrobatics, music, staging and movements were lively and dramatic.

We saw another opera, entitled *Azalea Mountain*, which concerned the struggle to establish a medical cooperative in a mountain area. It had all the elements of a western. Actors swung on ropes across the massive stage, and the grand finale was a masterpiece of acrobatics spiced with great humour. But the whole opera was pervaded by the inevitable overtones of the glory of the Revolution.

We were surprised at the lack of enthusiasm on the part of the Chinese audience. When I mentioned this to the guide, he remarked, "Everybody is sick of it. Only six operas are permitted to be performed, and everybody has seen them a dozen times. We are given tickets to go and it is wise to do so." All the old opera forms and traditional entertainment so much beloved by the masses had been replaced by the Gang of Four. Only drama and music devoted to promoting revolutionary ideals were permitted.

As we listened to enthusiastic briefings on impressive developments and increased production we were sometimes a little amused and even occasionally irritated by the continual propaganda. There was no doubt that workers were under pressure to produce. As we walked through factories and communes, we constantly saw the quotation, "Nothing is hard in this world if you have the determination to scale the heights."

Workers were organized into production teams, and posters and chalk boards highlighted those workers who surpassed their quotas or were the "outstanding worker of the week." Every year the state set a quota for each factory or commune, and it seemed the chief delight of the teams was to beat the quota. Clever diagrams of goals, flags, mountains and highways were mounted in one factory by a shock team organized to upgrade standards and encourage even greater achievements. No one seemed to be content to rest on past records: the Revolution had only begun and it must go forward. There was to be no slackening of the revolutionary spirit, and we were made conscious of this on every occasion.

18. Endings and Beginnings

On January 8, 1976, Chou En-lai died. Premier of China and Mao's chief lieutenant, Chou was beloved and respected by the people. But the Gang of Four rejoiced at his death. His prestige with the people had been a threat to their bid for power. They suppressed the outpouring of the nation's grief, and it was not until the end of the year, when films and stories became public, that the loving tributes of a nation were revealed.

Throughout 1976, the country was in ferment. Mao's health was failing and the Gang of Four seemed firmly in control. But when Mao died on September 7, 1976, a million people gathered in Beijing's massive Tiananmen Square for a "Mass Memorial for the Great Leader and Teacher, Mao Tse-tung." In spite of his questionable leadership in the last few years of his life and the obvious mistakes he had made, the nation mourned a hero. He was recognized as a great man who had completely turned a nation of a billion people onto a new path and fired it with a fierce determination to modernize and develop both its natural resources and its human potential.

When one is living in the midst of events, it is impossible to assess accurately their impact and direction. But there is little doubt that what had happened in China since 1949 changed the course of history. Mao Tse-tung, in spite of his failings, was a colossus of the twentieth century, whose determination redirected and transformed the lives of a quarter of the world's population, and whose ideas have challenged the structure and basic concepts of all society. It is for men like Chou En-lai and Mao Tse-tung that Stephen Spender's lines seem appropriate. In his poem "I Think Continually of These," Spender writes:

> I think continually of those who were truly great,
> The names of those who in their lives fought for life
> Who wore at their hearts the fire's centre
> Born of the sun they travelled a short while towards the sun,
> And left the vivid air signed with their honour.

The problem that lay before the Chinese people in 1976 was whether or not the concept of the new China could be maintained and carried forward. Spender continues:

> What is precious is never to forget . . . .
> Never to allow gradually the traffic to smother
> With noise and fog the flowering of the spirit.

The people of China had been enraged by the suppression of their mourning for Chou En-lai and with the death of Mao Tse-tung the wrath of the nation fell on the Gang of Four. Under the leadership of the new chairman, Hua Kuo-feng, the Gang of Four were arrested in October and their trials and subsequent imprisonment were world-wide news. The year 1976 saw the end of an era, and the Chinese people were as jubilant as if it were a second liberation. With the calling of the National Congress in 1978, we waited to see what new directions China would take.

Meanwhile, my own personal life began to change. Dick's declining health became very marked by the end of 1976, and in April 1977, cancer of the pancreas was confirmed. Together we explored new natural treatments which considerably prolonged his life and added greatly to his comfort. I gave up all my activities to devote to the demands of the therapy and for some time his health improved. We spent a very happy Christmas with the family in 1977. That eighteen months was a period of mutual growth in understanding, of greater perceptions of the meaning of life and death and a heightened awareness of a radical new holistic approach to health. Although the doctors had warned us that pancreatic cancer was almost incurable and exceedingly painful, the natural therapy made the illness so much more bearable that Dick was never hospitalized and died at home in August 1978, at the age of seventy-five — almost forty-four years after our joyful wedding in Canton.

Through the fall months I began to pick up the pieces and, among other interests, I found friends and work to do in the Canada-China Friendship Association. When a national federation of these CCFAs was formed in the spring of 1980, there was a need for a national tour director to coordinate and organize the growing demand for tours to be undertaken by the various friendship associations across Canada.

"Would you be willing to accept this volunteer position?" I was asked.

I was free to do so. I had experience with group travel, and my two trips to China in 1974 and 1976 had whetted my appetite for more. Little did I realize the magnitude of the job I was undertaking.

Quickly I put together a tour programme for 1981, searching the cross-country membership for leaders who had already been to China and had the knowledge and leadership ability to do the job. In the meantime an opportunity arose in the summer of 1980 to participate in a tour which included Inner Mongolia, and I jumped at the chance. In preparation, I made a study of a little-known and scantily documented area, and the trip proved fascinating.

Inner Mongolia, one of the four autonomous provinces of China, was originally part of the empires of Ghengis and Kublai Khan, stretching from Korea and the Siberian Steppes to India and Europe. Outer Mongolia is now an independent state and a member of the United Nations, but Inner Mongolia and the northwest provinces of Xinjiang and Gansu are part of China, although they retain their distinctive Turkish-Mongolian heritage. The nationalities who populate the northwest — largely Uighers, Kazaks and Wei — are more middle eastern in appearance, and together with the Mongolians, are almost universally Muslim.

Very few foreigners had visited this part of China up to 1980, and the children in particular eyed us with great curiosity. We found ourselves in a very different China, an area of wide open spaces, sparse population, different interests and customs. Many Han people, who form ninety-four percent of the Chinese population, had moved to Mongolia to help develop the area. But the province was designated an autonomous region, so the Mongolian people have controlling rights and their language, customs and religious beliefs are maintained.

On our first day in Hohhot, the capital of inner Mongolia, we were taken to a Nationalities factory where saddles and blankets, silver-handled hunting knives and decorative high leather boots were evidence of the life and culture. A visit to the Rodeo training grounds emphasized the place of the horse in the life of the people. We saw amazing performances of riders standing on their heads on the backs of racing horses and incredible feats of jumping and horsemanship.

Our next stop was an artists' school, where we were treated to a fine display of singing and dancing, Mongolian style. The colourful costumes, strange instruments, spirited dances and haunting songs of the rolling plains were a happy introduction to this strange new land.

But this was only the prelude to more exciting events. We were loaded on to two small buses with our overnight bags and started the climb through the mountains to the Grasslands. This was the Mongolia of the steppes, for centuries the breeding home of horses, and the grazing range of large flocks of sheep and goats which roamed the rolling, treeless hills. Small settlements of permanent mud-brick houses dotted the landscape, but the yurt was home to many families when they travelled with their herds in the summer months.

The yurt, a large tent of camel's hair felt, was supported by a sturdy framework that could be erected in a couple of hours and taken down in forty minutes. They were then easily packed on camels or in donkey carts and transported to the next grazing tract. The yurt was commodious with beautiful hand-woven hangings, carpets and cushions on the floor, a fire circle in the centre with a skylight for air and light, which could be closed for protection when needed.

We stayed overnight in the yurts, four of us to a tent, with ample room, clean, comfortable pallets and cozy quilts. A donkey cart arrived with jugs of water for the wash basins. Toilet facilities were outside close by.

On a second visit to the Grasslands a year or two later, we had an extraordinary and hilarious experience. As there was little to do on the vast plain after supper, I asked our guide if there was any possibility of some entertainment. Perhaps some of the guides or kitchen staff could sing or dance. The guide said he would see what he could arrange. I was hardly prepared for what ensued.

At the mess shack where we ate, there were six tables seating ten people each, three down each side of the room with a small open space in the centre. On one side our group of twenty-nine were seated. On the other side were various Chinese people, cadres from several units crossing the Grasslands on business, a few women, but mostly men stopping overnight on their way to confer with other towns and villages. When supper was finished our guide told us that the local cadre, a chunky, jolly fellow between fifty and sixty years of age, was arranging something, so we waited in anticipation. First of all, with a glass of powerful "maotai" (a scorching white wine), he went to our three tables singing a rollicking toast, in a rather raucous voice. Not to be outdone, one of our men who had a fine singing voice, toasted the other three tables with the drinking song from *The Student Prince*.

By this time the waitresses, who had been brought up on our buses to wait on our tables, had changed into Mongolian dress and were now dancing with the cadre and others joining in. Then, from out of the blue, appeared a man with an accordion who could play any tune we could hum. Two of the bus drivers agreed to a duet, and to everyone's amusement, one sang the tenor lead and the other, in falsetto, sang the female part.

"Now it's your turn," they announced.

Three of our couples agreed to do a polka accompanied by the versatile accordionist. Meanwhile we were hurriedly reviewing the procedure for doing the Virginia Reel which we presented, very creditably I'm sure, to the delight of the audience. After several more impromptu items the guide came to me and said, "Would you like to dance?"

I said I was sure we would, thinking that they were about to teach us some Mongolian folk dances. But to our amazement, the accordionist started up a fox trot, and a Chinese gentleman, who had been sitting watching proceedings very seriously all evening, walked across the room and asked me if I would dance. I was astonished but willingly agreed. He whisked me around the floor at a breathless pace and the accordionist kept going. When some others joined in, I wondered if I were dreaming. Were we really ballroom dancing in a mess shack in the middle of the Mongolian Grasslands where Ghengis Khan and his fierce warriors once held sway? Dancing continued until the cadre said that, since people had to be up early to start their journeys, we must end festivities. We went out into the warm, black night with the stars twinkling brilliantly overhead, and walked to our tents scarcely believing what had happened.

The next day we had a long drive across the steppes to tour the area where hay is grown for winter fodder, and where huge piles of dried animal dung are stacked for winter fuel in a treeless land.

Mongolia has a history and culture all its own. The Great Wall was built to keep the Mongol hordes from invading China proper, but in 1215 the Mongol army poured into the northern capital of Peking, looting, burning and massacring. The conquest was completed by Kublai Khan in 1279. He developed such an appreciation for Chinese civilization and culture that he transferred his capital to China, adopted a Chinese life style, and reigned more as a Chinese emperor than a Mongol Khan. However, after the death of Kublai Khan, the vast empire fell apart and Mongolian dominance ceased. Eventually the Manchus annexed Mongolia in 1636, and made it part of China when they established themselves as rulers of China in 1644.

In recent years the government, recognizing both the need for security in a sensitive region bordering the Soviet Union, and the benefits of a more stable grazing pattern for greater animal productivity, has assisted the herdsmen to organize people's agricultural communes. Pasture land has been fenced, irrigation installed and permanent settlements constructed. Industry has been introduced, particularly wool spinning mills to handle the raw product from the sheep. The production of iron, steel, coal and chemicals have also become important factors in the economy of the province.

Universities and scientific institutes have been established to specialize in subjects related to life in Mongolia, such as developing improved fodder grass and trees that will grow in harsh climates.

"Send us Canadian farmers to help us," we were told. "They understand our country best." Since then, some Mongolian farmers have spent a year living in Saskatchewan with their counterparts, and Canadian specialists have gone to Mongolia to advise and assist. At present, a young farmers' exchange has just been initiated between Saskatchewan and Mongolia. This vast northern province of China is fast becoming the heartland of productive animal husbandry.

19. Education in China

"Yat yuet chau hoi king kwan shi t'in (The sun and the moon appear, then male and female are created)," noisily intoned the primary class in Canton in 1904, as Mother heard them on her approach to the school.

"Shau sun chai ke gi kok yee hau ping tin ha (Begin with individual moral cultivation, then the ordering of the family, followed by the ruling of the nation which leads finally to the harmony of the universe)," chanted the grade threes as the Chinese masters put our afternoon classes at St. Hilda's school through their Chinese language studies.

"Wei run min foo wu (We serve the people)," lustily recited the young students in 1976, as we walked through their school. The content had radically changed but the technique, in certain respects, was the same. Class recitation is still an integral element in Chinese education, and memorization is very important.

An educational system is a good national barometer. The numbers who participate, the subjects taught and the teaching philosophy reflect the life style and attitudes of a country.

When my mother was involved in the schools in Canton in the early 1900s, education was chiefly classical. Only a very few girls attended school, arriving in covered sedan chairs or escorted by servants. The Confucian philosophy was pervasive, although the mission schools introduced Christian precepts which were committed to memory.

Confucian teaching was based on a rational social order which came about through an ethical approach grounded in personal cultivation. Political harmony and order flowed from harmony and moral order, which in turn was achieved by each person developing moral harmony within himself or herself. Hence, children were drilled in moral and ethical teachings, memorizing and repeating them until the ideals were indelibly imprinted on the mind as desirable standards of behaviour. The written word reinforced the spoken, and since Chinese characters were both artistic and complex, calligraphy was an art form. Hours were spent with brush and inkstone developing a writing style judged for its grace, elegance and well-proportioned aesthetic qualities.

Science had no place in education. A bitter battle had been waged in the 1860s, with an attempt to introduce science into the schools that trained scholars for government service. The conservative opposition insisted that the examination system was based on literature and not on technical subjects. Officials should be trained only in the classic principles of government and their application to a society where revered scholars grew six-inch finger nails to show their contempt for manual labour. Science was considered the concern of subordinates and should not be recognized as part of true learning.

By the turn of the century, however, some young men were being sent overseas for training, particularly in engineering and Western medicine. Sun Yat-sen, who led the movement that overthrew imperial rule, was a medical doctor who received his early education in a mission school and later trained in the West. Traditional education remained largely academic and classical.

Looking back at the school curriculum in St. Hilda's where I taught in the 1930s, I do not recall any emphasis on science. We had no science lab, no field trips, no one on staff who taught science, except one Chinese member who was a Cambridge graduate in mathematics and possibly taught a little theoretical science.

It was not until Liberation in 1949 that the importance of science and technology began to be appreciated, and China realized how far she lagged behind. And it is only since the Cultural Revolution and under the leadership of Deng Xiao-ping, that there has been an intensive drive to bring China into the scientific age. Thousands of students are being sent overseas to be trained in Western languages, science and technology, and schools in China are heavily stressing science geared to technology and economic and environmental development.

When the Gang of Four took over in 1966, they bitterly opposed any emphasis on scholarly accomplishment. Intellectuals in all fields were denounced as elitists who divorced theory from practice. Learn From the Peasants became a popular slogan. Workers, soldiers and peasants were invited to lecture and teach in the schools and universities, while professors and teachers were sent to the countryside. The standard of education fell drastically.

In 1974 in Hangzhou, I visited the Hsue Chun Junior-Senior Secondary School, which had fifteen hundred students and one hundred teachers and staff. Mr. Chiao, vice-chairman of the revolutionary committee, which during the Cultural Revolution was the governing body of the school, briefly laid out the policy of the school. "Proletarian leadership in the school has been strengthened," he said. "Before the Cultural Revolution the school was divorced from proletarian politics and from production and from the workers and peasants. Since 1968, this is no longer true. Over one hundred peasants and soldiers have been invited to give lectures in the school and our teachers are chosen from peasants, workers and soldiers. Serious efforts have been made to carry out Chairman Mao's policy of educating the student morally, intellectually and physically, to create a worker with a social conscience. Students organize to study Marxism, Leninism and Mao Tse-tung thought. The keynote is Keep Fit, Study Hard and Work Well, actively attempting to learn from Comrade Lei Fung (a model worker)."

Mr. Chiao went on to say that the school was now run in an "open door way," Students no longer studied behind closed doors, but spent time working on farms and in factories to relate school life to production and scientific development.

This type of briefing was typical of all the educational institutions we visited in 1974 and 1976. All students were required to do several months of field or factory labour. When we visited a College of Pharmacy, we found students working in the college factory, operating pill-making machines as part of their training. The trouble with this policy was that activities took so much of the students' time that scholastic studies were greatly curtailed. Professors, teachers, doctors, nurses and business people were expected to go to the countryside to assist with the harvest and participate in other types of labour. On several occasions, we found hospitals short of medical or nursing staff who had gone off to the countryside to do their stint of manual labour.

In theory, the idea of city dwellers having some experience in the countryside doubtless had value, but the practice had an ugly side. The intelligentsia were punished by being sent to the countryside for long periods, often under great hardships doing work to which they were unaccustomed and unsuited. Students frequently spent years in the countryside with little hope of returning to their homes or even seeing their families. After the fall of the Gang of Four, thousands of young people, forced to remain indefinitely on communes where they were frequently not wanted and only tolerated, returned to the city.

"Give us back our lost youth," they said, but it was too late. With sixty percent of the population under thirty years of age, the oncoming generation was taking their place, and many of the victims of displacement became bitter and cynical.

The breakdown of the educational system, the loss of skilled teachers and the alienation of the young people severely crippled the nation. Pure scientific research had been discouraged, even forbidden, and universities and colleges had been closed or drastically reduced in number.

Since the overthrow of the Gang of Four, schooling has been completely revised. Standards of scholarship have risen, teachers and professors who survived the hardships and cruelties of the Cultural Revolution have been re-instated and obligatory manual labour has been largely eliminated. Students now proceed with fulltime, uninterrupted studies.

College education, however, is as yet open only to a relative few. China has still to catch up with the great demand for teachers in a variety of fields. Foreign experts are warmly welcomed if they are willing to work cooperatively in the system. Hundreds of Westerners are teaching in China today as the demand for English is overwhelming. Millions listen daily to English radio and television lessons, and English has become a compulsory course in public schools.

In the summer of 1986, I was part of a unique experiment carried out by Yantai University in Shandong province. This new university, only a year old at the time, decided to offer a five-week English immersion course. I was asked to recruit seven or eight teachers from Canada for mid-July and August, to handle the eighty students expected. The response was so great that ninety-five students arrived. We taught four hours a day, six days a week. Each of us gave an evening lecture, and together, we conducted social evenings. The eager students, ranging from beginners in English to those quite fluent, came from all parts of China at great expense either to themselves or to the institutions which sent them. My class consisted of oil drillers, seismic and electrical engineers, a waitress, an office clerk, a librarian and various other personnel. Most of them came from the Shengli Oil Field and were sponsored by their company. When I asked them why they had come, they explained that they wanted to be able to read scientific journals and talk to foreign experts who visited the oil field from time to time.

The revolution in education in China over the last eighty years has been phenomenal. In 1903, the illiteracy rate was eighty-five percent. In 1933, it was probably between sixty and seventy percent. But by 1983, the illiteracy rate was estimated at only twenty-four percent, with ninety percent of the children having at least entered the first grade. My mother taught the favoured few whose parents could afford the fees and who considered education for girls worthwhile. In the thirties, I taught a wide range of girls, whose parents were able to pay fees or who were subsidized by the school for various reasons. Education was partly a matter of prestige and partly a practical method of acquiring the background and skills that would lead to useful work or a profitable profession such as nursing. But education was still for the few, and enterprising children of the lower classes were only able to get a smattering of training from socially responsible students willing to give volunteer classes to the poor.

With Liberation in 1949, education became free and universal. Adults flocked to night schools to learn basic reading and writing. It took some time for sufficient teachers to be recruited and trained and for schools to reach the remote areas, but today elementary and junior secondary schooling is compulsory. Not all rural areas have attained this standard, but the Department of Education is pressing for compliance. In April 1986, the National People's Congress passed a new "Law of the People's Republic of China on Compulsory Education." Eighteen articles lay down the details of the system which is free and compulsory, and provide for teacher training and the raising of the social status and material benefits of teachers. Copies of the law — six short pages — have been made available in English and make easy and interesting reading. Much has still to be done, however. To make sure that the millions of school-age children attend classes is a monumental task, which includes educating parents to keep the children in school when they could help on the farm.

Of even greater importance is the need to raise the social status and salaries of teachers. They tend to be so poorly paid that good students often shun teaching or are forced into the job against their will because of the shortage in the profession. I have heard physics graduates complain because they are sent to schools to teach English rather than being allowed to continue work in their own field.

The basic philosophy of education is stated as being the development of the student morally, intellectually and physically to become a worker with a social consciousness and a cultural understanding. The threefold thrust of moral, intellectual and physical excellence is the cornerstone of education in the new society.

The educational process begins at a very early age. Factories, communes and neighbourhood organizations have nurseries and kindergartens, since practically all women work outside the home. Women have sixty days maternity leave with full pay and then may bring their two-month-old baby to work with them. Trained nursery personnel care for the little ones, on a twenty-four hour basis, when shift work is involved, and the mother has time off for nursing and visiting her baby. Normally the child goes home with the mother each night, although in a few cases, they may go home only on week-ends if the mother must work nights and sleep during the day.

Men are slowly beginning to assume responsibility in the home. With the present drive for only one child per family, that child is precious and is looked after carefully by both parents. It is a common sight — particularly in urban areas — to see kindergartners riding with Dad on his bike on the way to school.

When the child is three years of age, he or she graduates into kindergarten, where the teachers' care and training establishes a security and rapport between the children themselves, and with the staff. I saw one little girl go up to her kindergarten teacher, whisper a question and then throw her arms around the teacher's neck and give her a hug. The result of the group experience is children who know how to play together, work together and yet act independently, and compete in games with friendship.

Concern has been expressed that children may become more attached to their kindergarten teachers than their parents. Perhaps to counter this criticism, emphasis is placed on the family. In the summer of 1984, I was standing by the door of a warehouse when I heard some children singing. Looking around, I discovered three five-year-olds singing a song they had learned that day in kindergarten. One of the mothers was sitting on a carton grinning at them as they sang "Mamma, Mamma," a song relating all the kind things Mamma did for her family.

The songs and dances provided for our enjoyment by the children are the warmest and most delightful experiences of our trips.

"I'm a little bus driver," sing four-year-olds, as they turn their chairs around and steer them. A little costumed "tomato" grows before our eyes as the gardeners sing and rake and hoe. The Uigher minority group of Xinjiang province is portrayed by eight charmingly costumed dancers, moving to the rhythm of their own tambourines and the drums and castanets of the other children.

Boys and girls are all trained in dancing and singing. Their graceful hand movements and their simple and rhythmic ballet steps are delightful and carry over into adult body movement.

One amusing incident at a kindergarten had our group laughing hilariously. Four little girls in white jackets came in and arranged four chairs. Four little boys followed, removed their hats and sat down as the children sang the Barber's Song. The girls clipped, with fingers working as scissors, and one of the boys had his false moustache shaved off. One of our bearded group members asked if he could get a haircut so the children delightedly repeated the song. When it came time for the removal of the moustache, the little girl barber gave our friend's beard a very vigorous tug, to his and everyone's prolonged laughter.

Moral values are strongly emphasized through song, dance and story. "One Phen" was a song about a single coin picked up by a child on the street and taken to the police as lost property. Another song was called "The Lost Handkerchief".

"I wish I could fly to Canada by plane to visit the Canadian children and bring them greetings from Chinese children," sang one little girl, who with the help of her friends, had composed the song for our visit. Her teacher had set it to a well-known tune. The children of China win the hearts of visitors, and the stories of their activities and entertainments are endless.

In many of the larger cities there are "Children's Palaces," extra-curricular activity centres where children go after school and on holidays for everything from games, drama, singing, accordion, violin, piano and ballet lessons to morse code, chess, first aid, conservation projects and almost any interest that can be named. Children have to take turns because they cannot all be handled at once, but those showing promise in music or dancing or singing are kept on at community expense to train for concert level performance.

Children enter the formal education system at six or seven years of age and must attend six years of primary school and three years of junior secondary. Organizations and individuals are prevented by law from employing school-age children or adolescents who should be in school.

Subjects in school consist of Chinese language, foreign language (chiefly English but sometimes Japanese or Russian), mathematics, physics, chemistry, history, geography, political theory, basic agriculture, physiology and hygiene, physical education, music and drawing. Physical culture is vigorously promoted, and children must participate in some form of games. Facial relaxation exercises are done in classes each morning to music on the loud speaker. This is designed to tone up the system and relieve eye strain which is particularly prevalent because of the concentration needed in writing Chinese characters.

My visits to secondary schools sometimes took the same form. I would listen to a class in English and then take time to visit with the students so that they could practise their often quite fluent English.

At one secondary school, the students gave a concert which was typical of the fine performances I saw in many centres. The first item was topical. In the summer of 1976, just before Mao's death and the fall of the Gang of Four, my group had arrived in Beijing where we had experienced the earthquake that flattened Tangshan, some ninety miles away. Using the earthquake as a subject, the students had composed a song which said in essence: "the earthquake was very great, but we will work to overcome disaster. We shall rebuild and go forward." Then, with no conductor but with perfect timing, the choir sang for us, accompanied by an accomplished student accordionist.

In the kindergartens and secondary schools we had frequently heard songs and dances of the minority peoples, as a spirit of concern and friendship for them is being fostered in the schools. Many of these minorities helped Mao and his followers as they passed through their territories on the Long March. When I travelled through Mongolia, along the Silk Road or to the far southwest, I was most interested in the development of education in these areas. The minority people who live there are encouraged to develop their own culture with provision for educational facilities in their own areas. This has been a gradual process, not always harmonious and one marked by neglect during the Cultural Revolution, but more and more there is a united effort to assist and develop these semi-autonomous areas. In 1984, special legislation defined their rights and privileges. Universities have been established which cater to research relating to local needs and to the encouragement of local leadership capable of meeting the demands of modern government, industry, agriculture and education.

I have frequently been asked about training for the physically and mentally handicapped. China is certainly moving ahead in this field. One specialized school I visited in 1976, was the School for the Deaf and Dumb in Canton. It had originally been set up in 1946 as a private school with high fees and a staff of seven for thirty students. After Liberation, the number of staff increased to seventy-seven, and 290 children were drawn from all over the city. Some lived close by, others walked a little distance, and some were picked up by bus each day.

Most of the children in this school were deaf-mutes on arrival, but according to the principal, seventy-six percent of the children regained all or partial hearing through acupuncture and were then taught to speak. Of that seventy-six percent, twenty percent recovered sufficiently to attend regular school and six graduates went on to become teachers. One-third of the children were born deaf, two-thirds were damaged at birth or through high fevers, bad home care or excessive prenatal use of medicines by mothers. Ever-expanding education was being undertaken to prevent prenatal and postnatal damage.

After graduation from this school the children were assigned to various jobs; the school appeared to find no difficulty in placing them. Attached to the school was a small farm and a sewing factory where students gained experience. I was taken to observe various classes: groups of students having their daily acupuncture period, children who had regained some hearing learning to pronounce words by repeating them after the teacher, groups reciting times tables and doing arithmetic on the board and classes and individuals reading aloud. Finally, an excellent programme of singing, dancing and instrumental work was presented by children eight to thirteen years of age, all of whom had regained their hearing and learned to speak and sing in the school.

A visit in 1988, to a deaf and blind school, was further evidence of China's concern for the handicapped. A fine orchestra of blind students presented several numbers for our enjoyment. But the most outstanding performance was that of a totally deaf girl, beautifully costumed, who presented an intricate East Indian dance to the music of a tape recorder she could not hear. Her only guide was the occasional inconspicuous indication of the rhythm or a movement by her teacher on the side line. A very dedicated staff gave us a warm welcome and we were presented with charming little folded baskets made by the younger deaf children of the school.

In Beijing there is a carpet factory where a large percentage of the workers are physically handicapped, some of them blind. Blind persons are also frequently trained to become excellent masseurs. On one of my trips, when eighteen of us asked for massage, six blind "doctors" were sent to our hotel and gave us each forty-minute workouts that were most relaxing and refreshing.

As I have noted in previous chapters, university students have always been in the vanguard of movements for political change and reform. Confucian philosophy is basic to Chinese culture. Confucius taught that the scholar was a superior man who, because of knowledge, must be a leader. Knowledge taught him what was right, and by living according to his knowledge he, his family and his nation would benefit.

Students have in many ways been the conscience of their country. Sun Yat Sen was a scholar who gathered students around him to challenge imperial power. They succeeded in toppling the imperial throne, but having no power base, they were unable to set up a democratic form of government.

Again in 1919, students acted as the conscience of their country when they successfully prevented the Chinese delegates to the Versailles conference from signing the Treaty of Versailles because of its unjust treatment of China.

During the Japanese invasion, it was the students who persistently demanded that Chiang Kai Shek stop harassing the Communists and concentrate on mobilizing the forces of China against the invaders.

In a smaller way, the students in my husband's school set up classes on Saturdays and holidays for the illiterate street children, and the girls in my school went out to the country villages to speak on public health. Another group of students took up the paving stones which covered the gutters in their streets and cleaned out the filth, as a lesson to the people of their village. There was a sense of responsibility that students owed something to their country and must offer leadership.

In November and December of 1986, big character posters appeared, and student demonstrations erupted in several large cities, although not to the extent of later protests. The actions of the students did, however, prompt the Beijing Review to issue in 1987, a free English-language booklet entitled "Student Unrest: What Is It All About?", which is well worth reading.

Some of the student complaints were recognized as legitimate. Undoubtedly accommodation and meals badly needed improvement. Students are often crowded into four- and six-bed dormitories which makes studying difficult and privacy impossible, and meals are often not adequate or nutritious. As one professor explained to me, college authorities have no knowledge of how to handle canteens: such matters are not considered their responsibility. Dining hall managers produce a meal for a fixed sum without much regard for the needs and physical well-being of the students.

The question of the "iron rice bowl" has also been simmering in China for some time and is manifesting itself in all walks of life. This phrase represents the idea that once a person has been given a position to which he or she is entitled, that person cannot be removed. Industry is beginning to review this attitude and to insist on productivity and responsibility as part of the right to a job, and universities and colleges are moving to establish the right to deny free education to those students who are lazy and unwilling to work once they have won for themselves a place at university.

But far more basic problems lie beneath the surface. The demand for freedom and democracy is a cry for a policy consistent with the promises made by the government in recent years. While peasants and labourers have benefitted greatly from reform, the intellectuals have not. Increases in remuneration for teachers fall far below those of the working classes, and there is little flexibility in the intellectuals' choice of work. University graduates are assigned jobs, and they become members of a work unit. If they are efficient and effective and want to move on to another position, they are frequently prevented from doing so by their work unit which refuses to release such a valuable worker. Frequently the jobs they are assigned are not closely related to their studies, are poorly paid and boring and worst of all offer little hope of advancement. Students are asking for more flexibility, more freedom of choice and better returns on their years of studies.

Students are, moreover, questioning the government's sincerity in its promise of reform. The government, by its crackdown and its dismissal of prominent liberal leaders, has created a credibility crisis in the intellectual community. The accusation of "bourgeois liberalism" appears to be a catchword used by anti-intellectuals to denigrate students and professors who dare to criticize ineptness and who participate actively in the call for reform.

It was the intellectuals who suffered so cruelly during the Cultural Revolution. Party officials seen unwilling to trust the men and women who have the willingness and capacity to carry out the economic, scientific and educational reforms necessary for China's modernization and progress. The embattled advocates of intellectual freedom are forced by the ideological conformists to retreat in fear of reprisals. China's credibility and progress is in question. With rising inflation and the failure of the government to grapple with some of the real problems in Chinese society, the students have become more and more vocal. They see inflation as a result of corruption. The gains being made in China's economy they say are being appropriated by leaders and their families. The students demand an end to corruption, an inquiry into the private possessions of top leaders and the abolition of nepotism that gives family members political plums.

To air their grievances the students have demanded freedom of speech. In the absence of a free press the only way they can vent their discontent is in demonstrations and marches.

Very few students really understand the meaning of the term "democracy." They know little about the workings of a multi-party system and elected legislatures; they do not realize the need for a legal system that stands behind a democracy. Democracy and freedom are not synonymous terms. When asked what they mean by democracy, the answer is often "the right to speak out, to make choices and to be able to print the truth." These are freedoms. Granted, they are the adjuncts of a true democracy, but by themselves they do not constitute a democratic society.

The students in the May 1989 protest were struggling to gain freedom. Many of them see the affluence of the West, which they equate with democracy. They fail to realize that much of Western wealth is built on the backs of underprivileged nations, and that affluence has produced high crime rates, promiscuity, consumerism and waste.

The spirit of materialism has grown rampant in China. When a member of our group said to a student that money wasn't everything, his reply was, "Oh yes it is."

We cannot fault them for wanting a higher standard of living, but along with that must go other reforms. Economic reform has soared but legal, social and educational reforms lag far behind. Unless they soar hand in hand, there cannot be true democracy.

The government sees the students' demands as unrealistic and threatening to the socialist system on which the new China is founded. They feel that the lack of experience and the idealistic demands of young people who have not experienced the bitterness of the past and cannot see the pitfalls of the present, are dangerous shortcomings. They cannot allow the students to progress. With a billion people to govern, the government sees stability as essential.

The students' demands pose a threat to those in power, and the reaction of the authorities is evidence of their fear. Unless the government sees the need for understanding and dialogue with youth, the situation looks bleak. Coercion and the outrageous brutality which occurred in Tiananmen Square in June of 1989, is not the answer to the problems inherent in China's educational system. The country's future may well be jeopardized by its leaders' inability to free the intellectuals to carry out the reforms and development China so sadly needs in other than economic fields.

20. Health Care

The doubling of Chinese life expectancy from thirty-five years to seventy within forty years is, to me, an extraordinary achievement. It is undoubtedly an impressive tribute to the nation's gains in the medical and public health fields since 1949.

China had a vast store of medical knowledge gathered during its five thousand year history. Traditional medicine dates from primitive society's stone needle acupuncture to a highly developed philosophy of medicine that has evolved through the centuries. Hundreds of years before Christ, books of physiology, surgery, and anaesthesia were produced in China. During the third century A.D., tuberculosis, smallpox, beriberi, hepatitis and plague were identified and treated. Long before Europe had any such thoughts, a text on forensic medicine had been written.

But in spite of all this accumulated knowledge, treatment was reserved for the few. There was practically no access to medical help for the masses. Medical missionaries did contribute much to the alleviation of suffering and to the training of medical personnel in the areas where they worked, but the need was so great that their contribution was inadequate.

Women bore large families in the hope that a few children, particularly boys, would survive to care for their parents in old age. But a mortality rate of seventy-five percent amongst children was not uncommon.

When I walked down the streets in Canton in the thirties, children covered with sores and scabs lay on the sidewalk while mothers pleaded for handouts, and emaciated and deformed creatures crouched by the side of the road begging for pennies. Files of blind persons hanging on to each other stumbled pathetically along the street chanting their request for alms. Children defecated in the gutters, and the stench of the "honey carts" (tanks picking up the daily quota of human excrement) filled the night air. Each morning dead bodies were picked up on the steps of the City Hall or in alleys and under bridges — the poor who had died that night of malnutrition or disease with no hope of help. Human life was cheap.

"Did you ever consider where the word 'shanghaied' came from?" a Chinese woman asked me one day when I was travelling in northern China. I admitted I hadn't given it much thought. "I'll tell you," she said. "Someone would come from Dairen or one of the other northern ports to recruit dockworkers in Shanghai. Men would be seized and forced to go to the harbour cities. Their lives were, as we say, 'worse than that of a horse or an ox'. Sixty dockworkers lived in one room, and in the winter the water froze in the basin. Roofs were so low, the workers could barely stand up, and they were packed so tightly, they could only roll over in bed together. They worked fifteen hours a day and every day someone died from hunger, accident or illness."

The word "shanghaied" took on new meaning for me.

"In one year," she added, "out of 3,000 dock workers taken from Shanghai, 2,900 of them died, and another boatload was shanghaied."

When Liberation came in 1949, one of Mao's chief dictums was embroidered on banners, painted on walls and uttered in speeches: Of all Things People are the Most Precious. Applying this to the field of health, medical training had high priority.

In the early years of the new regime, doctors and hospitals tended to be concentrated in the cities. In 1965, however, Mao called on the health services to step up their work in the countryside, and a vast program of rural development began. During this period, rural medical co-ops came into being. At the same time, the first barefoot doctors appeared. These paramedics worked alongside their peers in the rice fields, acting as part-time first aid and basic medical workers. The term "barefoot doctor" implied an intimate relationship with the masses, as it applied both to first aid workers in the rice fields and to paramedics in fur-lined boots in the mountains of Tibet or on the plains of Mongolia. The term remained in use until the end of the seventies.

After a Peking medical team had traversed the Badin Jaran Desert to visit forty-two families in an 8,000 square kilometre area, one old herdsman remarked, "If we had searched the whole area for a doctor in the old society we would never have found one. But today, Chairman Mao sends doctors to this remote place to look for us."

The system of employing barefoot doctors grew out of the acute need for medical personnel. Someone interested in health would begin by gathering herbs from the hillside and studying their uses. A desire to learn more was followed by a visit of several weeks or months to the nearest medical centre to learn the basics of first aid and the giving of injections. Back in the commune or factory, the barefoot doctor resumed his or her work but was on call. If a mobile unit came to the area, the barefoot doctor would assist and, at the same time, benefit from further training. Eventually this paramedic could treat ordinary and frequently recurring illnesses, give acupuncture and even handle more complicated emergency cases. Some assisted at surgery and anaesthesia, and if they displayed real skill and a spirit of service, they might be recommended to continue their training to become full-time health workers, midwives or full-fledged doctors.

In the dozens of village clinics I visited, the emphasis is on traditional medicine. Drawers of herbs line the wall and acupuncture is offered universally. The government also issues injections and some medicines to these clinic so that they are easily available to everyone. Larger hospitals for surgery and more advanced treatment are located in every district, and, of course, in every town and city.

The cost of medical service is not completely free. Half the charges are paid by the agricultural, industrial or community unit the patient belongs to, and half are paid by the state. In the unit, the adult pays a small sum annually or semi-annually, and children often contribute a few cents per month in school. Charges are made for operations, but the patient pays only one or two dollars as his or her share.

As I am oriented to naturopathy and herbal medicine, I was intensely interested in Chinese traditional medicine. Consequently, I organized a tour in 1984 that would spend some time in Heilongjiang Traditional Medicine College, founded in 1959 in the North China city of Harbin. Nineteen of us left in May, and after a visit in Beijing, we went on to five days in Harbin, four of which were spent in classes and lectures and tours at the hospital and sanatorium connected with the college. The college had 3,000 students with a staff of 300 in three departments of Traditional Chinese Medicine, Acupuncture and Pharmacy.

On the first morning of our visit, we were shown an excellent video outlining the history and philosophy of Chinese traditional medicine going back to primitive times. The idea of "yin and yang" — the opposites that must be balanced for perfect health — was clearly developed. A tape and some slides on methods of diagnosis followed, and then the vice-president, fluent in English, presented an enlightening talk that expanded on the visual presentation.

In the afternoon, we were introduced to Chinese Materia Medica, the branch of medical science that deals with substances used for the cure or prevention of disease. Included in this presentation was an excellent paper on herbs, beginning with the history of a wise chieftain, who taught about medicinal herbs 5,000 years ago, and was known as "a divine husbandryman." Over the years, many collections of herbal remedies and information were recorded. The greatest name in this field is Li Shi Zhen (1518-1593), who completed an astonishing encyclopedia of fifty-two volumes which took twenty-seven years to finish. The text was illustrated with 1,100 pictures of herbal plants which the author himself painted. This text is still the basis for herbal medicine in China.

I recalled my visit to a college of pharmacy several years previously, when we passed through endless corridors of mounted plants and jars of herbs. Again in a hospital, I had taken a picture of a kitchen, where herbal remedies were simmering or steeping before being poured into the hundreds of thermos bottles lined up and waiting to be carried to patients. In that same hospital I was shown the medical charts of three patients admitted with appendicitis. All patients on admission were informed of their case and shared in decisions. These three were given the option of an operation or traditional herbal remedies, and all three chose the latter. Very careful records were kept of the patients' temperatures and general condition and if there had not been an immediate reduction of fever, surgery would have been indicated. But in all three cases, herbal remedies disposed of the problem and the patients were discharged.

The morning of the second day of our course was spent studying "chigong," a deep breathing technique used for healing and strengthening the body, a system 4,000 years old and considered a precious legacy. "Chi" is difficult to translate but can probably best be described as "vital energy" or "life essence." If chi is not in the right balance, the body is out of kilter and illness occurs. Chigong has always been part of Buddhist, Taoist and Confucian belief, and is taught as essential to mental tranquillity and physical well being.

In 1955, the first deep breathing sanatorium was set up in Tangshan and, by 1978, clinical research in the field was proceeding all over China. In some cases, chigong has even been found to be useful as an anaesthetic.

After softly and slowly attempting some of the deep breathing exercises, we tried to feel "chi," reaching along the channels to our solar plexus and even the soles of our feet. We could appreciate the long hours of practice and concentration needed to master this fascinating healing and tranquillizing process.

More active study followed in the afternoon, as we were led out of doors, and the College Master of Tai Chi guided us through tai chi body movements. The exercises looked simple but were very precise and demanded great control.

During the Han dynasty (202 B.C. - A.D. 220) the "Five Animal Games" were devised to imitate the tiger, deer, monkey, bear and crane, and tai chi developed from these movements to increase circulation and channel vital energy throughout the body. The "chi" in tai chi is the same "chi" as in chigong, and the two processes are closely allied. Tai chi is a discipline of the life force to produce a flowing, balanced movement through the body which allows the mind and spirit to absorb chi energy, release tension and regenerate, balance and unify the body and mind.

We were asked to empty our minds, to get rid of self-consciousness and expectations and concentrate on the movements as we followed our teacher. Over and over we practised the first set of movements. We promised ourselves we would continue to practise daily. A week or so later, when we were in the city of Hangzhou, we walked to the park near our hotel at 6:00 a.m. The park was full of groups and individuals practising tai chi from the simplest forms to highly advanced movements. One expert spotted our small group. Smiling, he motioned to us that he would guide us through the movements. We lined up and he patiently trained us for nearly half an hour, reviewing the lessons we had started at the college in Harbin.

On the third day of our introduction to traditional medicine, we came to the fascinating study of acupuncture. Like all the other traditional medicine techniques, acupuncture has a long history. Archaeological research shows that bin shu (stone acupuncture) began in the primitive society of the stone age using stone needles. Later, sets of needles dating from 475 B.C. have been discovered.

During the Han dynasty, an imperial medical college was established with four departments, one of which was acupuncture, and the practice of this technique spread to Korea, Japan, Southeast Asia and India and finally to Europe in the sixteenth century. Now, over one hundred countries use acupuncture and moxibustion — the application of herbs to the upper tip of the needle which are ignited and burn slowly, sending heat through the needle to aid in healing.

Much clinical research has been done on acupuncture, and curative effects have been authenticated in 300 common diseases as well as numerous unusual and emergency situations. Our lecturer listed many illnesses treated by acupuncture and pointed out that in neural and mental cases, the practice is most successful.

Several patients volunteered to appear at our class. We met a young man who had had facial paralysis, but now had full use of the facial muscles after acupuncture treatment. Two older people, one who had experienced left side paralysis and the other a stroke, walked into our classroom and submitted to an acupuncture treatment to display how they had been rehabilitated.

Acupuncture anaesthesia is now widely known throughout the world. I have seen a major operation performed while the patient was conscious and able to chat with the operating staff. Acupuncture is also used during pregnancy to prevent nausea, to correct an improperly positioned fetus, and during delivery to suppress pain and offer stimulus to birth.

I recalled my visit to the deaf and dumb school where children regained partial or complete hearing with acupuncture. I remembered experiences on previous tours. One of our members was very uncomfortable with bursitis, but two acupuncture treatments on the trip cleared it up, and ten years later it has not reappeared. A student on another trip suffered temporary heat exhaustion while visiting a commune. The clinic attendant immediately applied acupuncture, and the girl felt better than she had for several days in the intense heat spell we were experiencing.

To complete our brief look at acupuncture, we were taken to the acupuncture clinic in the hospital attached to the college, and several of the group benefitted from treatments for bursitis, an ear problem and arthritis. It would never have occurred to us, when we lived in China in the thirties, to go to a Chinese doctor for acupuncture or herbal treatment. Today however, acupuncture is becoming very popular in the West, and many herbal remedies have proved their efficacy. I have personally used both extensively in recent years to great advantage.

Following the acupuncture session we completed our course with a look at massage and its uses. Chinese medicine recognizes twelve pulses and considers the regulation of the pulse as the beginning of the healing process. This can often be brought about with massage. The many and varied methods of massage were demonstrated and we were encouraged to use some of the simple procedures. Several of us benefitted from some vigorous massage treatments given by the experts.

The last day of our course was spent visiting one of Sun Island's seven sanatoriums and the College Hospital. Sun Island was a pleasant extensive park area on an island in the middle of the wide Songhua River which flowed past the city of Harbin. Here, various industrial unions had sanatoriums where they sent their members to recuperate after an illness or operation. In the 780-bed Harbin Workers Union Hospital, we saw patients participating in many therapies: tai chi, water, wax, music and physio. They also enjoyed films, library facilities, recreation rooms, boating or swimming in the river, or just walking among the fragrant flowers and leafy trees considered part of the healing process.

Care in the sanatorium is free to union members. Smaller factories or rural organizations may contract for a fixed number of beds for their patients. Individual patients can be referred by doctors and pay a small fee.

The staff was most interested in us as Canadians, and in the introductory briefing made a strong plea for help from Canada for more modern technology and an exchange of ideas for peaceful ends.

In the afternoon, we visited the busy hospital attached to the College and saw massage and acupuncture clinics, laser machines, patients enjoying music therapy, a never-ending stream of out-patients and the busy pharmacy which dispensed both herbal remedies and modern drugs.

With the reinstatement of traditional medicine as a viable part of medical treatment, the two streams of healing have been brought together. Doctors in both fields of Western and traditional medicine have formed a combined association. Interesting research is being carried on to discover the scientific basis for the obvious success of much traditional medicine, and to integrate it into the whole medical scheme.

Paralleling the growth and development of traditional medicine is a phenomenal expansion of allopathic medicine and hospital care facilities. I have visited an outstanding institution, the Beijing Children's Hospital, founded in 1959. It is a very comprehensive complex of paediatrics, with departments of medicine, surgery, infectious diseases, traditional medicine, acupuncture, ear-eye-nose and throat, orthodontics, and all the backup departments of pathology, radiology and so forth. Outpatients number up to 3,000 per day; I saw throngs in the halls and waiting rooms. One of the major thrusts of this hospital is preventative work. All children in the schools in the area are checked by the staff, and home calls are made on all new-born babies within one month of birth. Children under a year then have a check-up twice yearly and children in nurseries and kindergartens at least once a year, with nutrition information given to the parents. Immunization programs are also an important feature. Every year doctors and medical teams are sent to the countryside to assist local medical personnel and to upgrade local doctors. The teaching and nursing school attached to the hospital also brings in medical workers from rural areas for training and practical experience.

There is a growing international exchange of medical information. A number of medical groups have gone to China from Canada and other Western countries to hold seminars and discussions with their Chinese counterparts, and to demonstrate and watch demonstrations in an interchange of ideas and methods.

The success of China's health programme has spawned a problem that is now being tackled — the phenomenal growth in the population. The doubling of the population since 1949 to its present assessment of approximately 1,200,000,000 poses enormous problems. A campaign for late marriages, widespread dissemination of birth control information, free abortion, and the guarantee of old-age security (eliminating the need for large families to care for the elderly), have contributed to a dropping birth rate. But with sixty percent of the population under thirty years of age, the number of women capable of bearing children has led the government to insist on a rule of one child per family. This policy in itself leads to the problem of the only child, who tends to be spoiled by parents and grandparents, and couples are faced with the dilemma of which parents will be cared for in their old age. The answers are not easy and the next decades are crucial.

21. The Rural Picture

In every developing country in this century, the cry has been "Land Reform." China was no exception. Before 1949, most of the land was owned by a few who lived off the peasants they exploited. Landowners, in walled compounds with extensive courtyards, were waited upon by numerous servants and lived luxuriously on hoarded supplies taken as rent from the peasants. Peasants paid from half to as much as three-quarters of their crop in rent, leaving little for food and often no seed grain for the following year. Needing capital to carry on their farms, they were obliged to borrow from their landlords who were also the money lenders. Exorbitant interest rates crippled the peasants still more. Unable to repay escalating loans, they forfeited their land. Displaced and homeless, they were forced to work for the landowner for a pittance, or drift from place to place as homeless labourers.

A few independent small farmers survived and became known as "rich peasants" because, unlike the landowners, they actually worked on their land.

With Liberation, the land was taken over by the state and redistributed. The wealthy landowners were naturally outraged, and the transition was not without violence.

"How did the landlords react when this land was taken over by the State?" I asked the chairperson of one commune.

"One landlord behaved quite well," she explained. "He was deprived of his political rights at first, but he was willing to work with the peasants and rehabilitate himself. Now he has had his rights restored and he is one of us. In fact, his experience was useful and he works on our management committee. The second landlord didn't react very well and was still labelled a landlord, but he was very old so we gave him a place to live. We kept him under supervision until he died of old age. But the third landlord resisted all our efforts to reform him. He refused to work with us, and after Liberation he killed several peasants. The people were so angry with him that they killed him."

The story Mrs. Ho told me in 1981 was typical of the experience of many rural people of China who make up eighty-five percent of the population.

"When we were first married," she said, "we had a small piece of land which we rented from the landlord. At first we raised wheat, but we had to sell it all to live. Even our next year's seed went for rent. So my husband and I and our seven children had to live on sorghum. But we could not make a living and eventually we lost everything. We were turned out of our house with nothing but my husband's carrying pole. we lived by begging. We had no house to live in. We just depended on any help we could get or occasional work.

"But fortunately, Liberation came and we were given land. By 1956, we had five rooms for our family. Now four of our children are working away from home and three are still here with us."

I looked around the room. It was a pre-liberation house with mud floors hardened and polished to the consistency of wood. It was simple but Mrs. Ho glowed with pride.

"See," she said. "I have a clothes closet, a sewing machine, a clock, a watch, a radio and nice dishes." She proudly showed me pictures of her children and then added, "My body doesn't ache any more because I have a warm, dry home. In the past the rain brought worry. It didn't matter whether we were inside or outside because the thatch roof had so many holes in it. Now the roof is fixed and I have a stove to keep me warm in winter. And today we have steamed bread made with wheat, and noodles that we make in our commune factory. Oh, we have so much to thank Chairman Mao and the Party for."

A mud floor, a rain-proof roof, a stove and a chance to make a living.

We went outside and she showed me her son's new house. He was soon to be discharged from the army and was to be married. "Isn't it beautiful?" said Mrs. Ho as we inspected the neat little brick house with tile roof and cement floor next door to her home.

At this point, a young man joined us and offered to show me the commune projects. We started off on a tour of the farm. With obvious pride he demonstrated what they had done with this once rather barren land. "Together we have built reservoirs instead of letting the rainwater drain away," he explained, "and we found springs on the hills so we piped the water for irrigation." We walked through a peach orchard, large piggeries, cattle stalls and a factory where commune members were building furniture from trees they had planted on the formerly barren hillside.

"You see that hillside," said my guide. "Nothing used to grow there, but now it produces timber for us. There's one barren section," he pointed out, "but we've left it like that to remind our children of what it was like before Liberation."

Unlike this one, some communes were not entirely devoted to agriculture. I visited one on the east coast which had a variety of enterprises. Half of the men were farmers and half were fishermen. Some of the women were engaged in agricultural work, but the majority did piecework embroidery for a factory in a nearby city.

In all these communities, provision is made for pre-schoolers to be cared for — babies in creches and the older ones in kindergarten. Some children still remain with grandparents, but parents are encouraged to send the children to the community kindergarten, particularly now that so many families have only one child and there is a need for children to work and play with other children.

Communes grew out of the need for vast projects of irrigation, diking and reclamation which could not be done by individuals. In 1949, land was taken over by the state and parcelled out to individuals, but within a year or two, farmers were encouraged to form Mutual Self-help Teams. By 1953, co-ops came into being when farmers used their land as shares and began cooperative ventures in irrigation and other communal programs. Then even a larger and more centralized programme was needed to tackle extensive developments including diking, electrification and the organization of district schools, clinics and hospitals. Communes, some as large as 70,000 people, came into being and production rose dramatically.

The smallest unit of the commune was the production team which was usually the village or settlement. The team appointed representatives to the brigade, which helped to coordinate production and organize services. Brigades then shared in the overseeing of the whole commune by sending delegates to the committee that planned and organized land development, projects, schools, hospitals and local security. Communes also interacted provincially and even nationally with other communes in an endeavour to bring about a rational development.

By the late 1970s, however, individual initiative began to question the commune system. Rather than be assigned to a job according to an overall plan, some farmers began to urge the government to allow them to contract to farm a specific area, pay the allotted produce or tax to the state and then be free to sell anything above that allotment for themselves in a free market. Trial districts were organized, specified areas were allocated for free markets, farmers' incomes grew and urban centres benefitted from the large supply of fresh produce brought to the markets. By the mid-1980s, the contract system had taken over.

But this development is not without its problems. The commune disappeared, as the family contract system emerged and townships replaced the communal organization. Social welfare and health institutions suffered to some extent, and the lack of central planning had serious effects. One of the consequences has been, in some parts, a critical shortage of grain, because farmers have elected to grow fruit or other crops that produce greater returns or require less arduous work. Also, as townships allocated more funds to commercial and sideline ventures, arable land has gone out of cultivation and irrigation and water conservation have been neglected. The sense of cooperation for the common good has been undermined to some extent, with much more emphasis placed on individual advancement rather than on community involvement.

There are still areas where improvement in living standards is slow. The deserts of the northwest, the intense cold of the extreme north, the dry winds of the plains and the extensive mountainous regions make development difficult. Then, too, old customs die hard. Herders still use portable camels' hair felt yurts which can be erected and dismantled quickly. The yurts are more suitable homes, at least for the summer when they are moving their herds across the northern and western plains. Mud bricks are also easier to make and build with on the treeless steppes or mountain slopes.

The government, however, has laid plans to assist in these regions and to develop untapped resources. With the spread of education and the training of local leaders, rural standards are rising everywhere. Research into new methods and new crops and the introduction of industry into the rural areas to supplement the income of the population have all contributed to a new and better life for China's countryside.

Returning each year to China, I have seen great changes and developments. In the cities the urban workers now talk about "the rich farmers." Certainly the rise in the standard of living in rural areas is phenomenal. In Shandong province, I was entertained in farmers' two-storey brick houses with small balconies and airy bedrooms and, in some cases, newly installed three-piece bathrooms and small washing machines. In other equally richly endowed areas, progress is similar, and foreign visitors may now stay overnight or longer in farm homes and enjoy the hospitality of the friendly rural workers.

It is becoming increasingly difficult in some cases to separate the rural and town communities. In April of 1989, I visited the Chang Qing (Evergreen) Township which is a mixture of agriculture and industry. Of the total labour force of 9,980, about 1,660 work in agriculture. The remaining workers are engaged in a printing shop, an Italian-Chinese joint enterprise refrigerator factory and a hotel. Others work in greenhouses which act as experimental stations and supply the city with tomatoes, peppers and cucumbers while doing research. There are plans for a joint enterprise with Hong Kong for setting up an automobile repair shop and for a gas station, glass and chemical factories and a textile factory. Profits from the enterprises are shared with the agricultural workers so that incomes are levelled off. Farmers are also free to sell their produce to the workers. A medical plan covers all who participate in either farm work or business enterprises, and money is allocated for cultural and recreational facilities.

One of the concerns of this type of development is that farm land is being taken over for industrial enterprises. To maintain a balance in a country that must feed a billion people each day, is a momentous problem.

22. *Aspects of Industry*

Industry in pre-Liberation China was grossly underdeveloped. Textiles and coal and iron extraction were the basic industries. No car or truck manufacturing existed, and what industry had developed in the rich mineral areas of Manchuria, had been largely introduced and controlled by the Japanese.

"When Liberation came," the manager of the Jinan Auto Works told me, "there wasn't a plant in China that built trucks. We had simply been a service industry for repairing military vehicles for Chiang Kai-shek and later for the Japanese. But in 1954, we were told we were to be given one hundred technicians and workers and one hundred days to design a truck and a plant for constructing trucks. We set to work night and day without stopping. We planned and designed and built until we finished the job on time."

He looked proudly round the large construction area. Twenty shining new vehicles stood in the yard outside; others were moving through the assembly line. Overhead was a huge banner which read "Nothing is hard in this world if you have the determination to scale the heights."

"See those trucks," he said pointing to half a dozen oil tankers. "After the auto works were built we couldn't get regular oil deliveries for our machines, so we designed these oil carriers to service our own plant. Now they are used all over China."

A woman who looked to be about twenty-eight years old, but whom I discovered later was forty, was introduced to me as the director of the workshop.

"Sixty percent of the workers in my shop are women," she said, "and in the whole factory women represent thirty percent of the total work force."

We watched a young woman operating a huge crane which ran along a track at roof level lifting steel and heavy equipment. "That young woman," she said pointing to an attractive machine operator, "designed an automated machine which produces thirty springs a minute instead of the original manual operation of twenty an hour."

As in other factories, the workers had free medical care, living quarters for which in 1974, they paid five yuan ($2.50) a month including water, electricity and furniture. Single people paid the equivalent of twenty-five cents a month for dormitory rent. Nurseries and kindergartens on the factory property cared for little ones, and schools in the district handled the older children.

In Beijing in 1974, our group visited an electrical factory, where we were warmly greeted with coloured chalk board signs reading "Welcome to our friends from Canada." Beside a beautiful drawing of trees and hills were the words "May our friendship with Canada be as tall as the pines and as long lasting as the mountains."

We were shown products ranging from electrical wire to immense turbines. Huge packing cases caught my eye and I was surprised to see them addressed to Tanzania, Kenya and other developing countries. The guide noted my interest.

"We share our output with our friends in other underdeveloped countries," he explained.

Again we found that workers participated in improvements. A woman proudly showed us her invention, an automatic method of covering wires that sped up production and made the old hand process unnecessary. The technicians had perfected her idea and now all she had to do was push a button and the operation was quickly completed.

At the time of Liberation, the state had taken over all industry, but obviously had no ready-made managerial staff to place in command. In the case of well-established businesses, those managers willing to cooperate with the new regime were left in positions of authority so that there would not be a complete breakdown in industry.

In the early days of the Revolution, China also received a great deal of help from the U.S.S.R. in personnel, technical information and materials. But in the late 1950s, the Russians broke with the Chinese, pulled out their experts, tore up plans and contracts and left China to her own devices.

"Maintain independence, rely on your own initiative," Mao pronounced, and the nation did. I heard the story of the famous Nanking Bridge when we visited that city and walked across the beautiful structure.

For decades the people of Nanking had wanted a bridge over the Yangtze River. Russia had drawn up the blueprints and promised the necessary steel which China was not yet producing. When the break came, the transportation ministry, cadres, workers and technicians got together and re-designed the bridge. The steel and iron industry experimented until they were finally able to produce the right kind of steel. Divers probed the river bed and designed piers to cope with the different land formations under the water. The state invested millions of dollars, and the bridge was literally built from scratch in ten years (1956-1966). It is a wide, double-decker construction, one mile in length, carrying railway traffic on the lower level and normal road traffic above, with three miles of elevated approaches. Carved stone statues, depicting the workers who made this project possible, stand midway along the bridge. An issue of stamps hailed the achievement. The story is a national epic, so well known, we found kindergarten children building a remarkably good imitation of the bridge with their blocks.

One of the most dramatic stories of development is one I have seen only in a private documentary film called *The Saga of the Red Flag Canal*. Linhsien County in Honan Province, with its thin, stony soil, had perpetually suffered from acute water shortage, drought and the consequent starvation. In the past the attitude had been: "mountains do not move and rivers have their courses. Man cannot change nature."

But the people of Linhsien County changed that saying to: "rearrange the mountains and rivers of Linhsien." So they blasted the tops and sides of 1,250 hills, excavated 134 tunnels, dammed the unruly Changho River and directed its waters through the Taihang Mountains into the Red Flag Canal to irrigate 100,000 acres of farmland.

The sight was incredible: 40,000 people at one time fanned out from the villages to blast and remove rock, fill in ravines, build tunnels, reservoirs, roads, bridges and aqueducts. Many of the tools were fashioned out of their own simple equipment. When blasting powder ran out, they made more out of chemical fertilizer. Everyone was involved, even Granny Chang, who trudged to a work site every day with refreshing drinks and bundles of shoes and shoulder pads she had mended for the builders.

Making use of the water overflow along the canal, the people built small hydro power stations — twenty-two in all — providing power for pumps, machines and lighting.

I rejoiced with Granny Chang and the villagers as I sat and watched on film "the day of jubilation." Women in holiday dress, grey-haired elders, excited children, men and women of all ages gathered to watch as the musicians played. When the sluice gates opened and the water poured through, cheers and songs burst forth. Like many of the observers, I had a lump in my throat and tears in my eyes as I saw their dream come true, a dream they had brought to reality by incredible cooperation and dedication.

In many areas, industry is being developed to process local products. In 1982 in Huhhot, the capital of Inner Mongolia, I saw three huge new woollen mills producing gabardines and other materials from the wool of thousands of sheep that range the Mongolian plains, as well as boots and jackets from the hides. Huge petrochemical plants are being built, often in the countryside in order to distribute the workers in areas outside the already overcrowded cities. Living quarters for the workers surround these rural based plants, with rice paddies or wheat fields often crowding right up to the very edge of the industrial complex.

My contact with the summer students from the Shengli Oil Fields when I taught at Yantai in the summer of 1986, made me realize the extent of the oil industry. They showed me pictures and told me of the immense complex in which they worked. China is now self-sufficient in oil production and is able to export some to Japan and underdeveloped countries. But as China industrializes and the standard of living rises, more and more pressure will be put on both offshore and land exploration to develop this national resource. Oil has been discovered off Hainan Island at the southern tip of China and its resources are to be tapped in the near future.

In Maanshan in the spring of 1989, flowers, fruit and a large welcome sign greeted our group at the large steel mill. The company running the mill operates on a contract system with its five factories, each producing a different product. In 1986, the company was criticized for its poor quality, so it set out to reach the world standard set for steel wire and rods. As they expressed it: "with the double wings of quality and efficiency we have achieved our purpose." Attached to the factory are cooperatives that make spare parts, cut up and recycle waste and develop small industries related to the large mill. It is worth noting that the management pointed out they are working to overcome pollution caused by the factory.

But not all industry is heavy duty or mechanical. Millions of people are engaged in the arts and crafts industries which remain essentially labour intensive. I have visited innumerable factories, but have never ceased to marvel at the skill of men and women who spend their days designing and creating the exquisite art objects for which China is justly famous.

China has had a tradition of fine pottery and porcelain for thousands of years, and the art continues to flourish. I had the opportunity to visit Zibo, called the porcelain capital of China, and brought home several delicate samples of unique glazes. Closely allied to this art is the making of cloisonne, whose fine wire fillets spread in patterns over an enamel surface require a steady hand and sharp vision.

The art of carving has also survived from primitive time, with wood, jade, turquoise and bone still fashioned in every conceivable shape and design.

Weaving and embroidery are so firmly ingrained in Chinese culture, that the country's factories produce an endless variety of products from beautiful handmade rugs to dainty silk embroideries.

I found a visit to a paper-cutting factory a fascinating experience. No one who has been to China can have failed to admire the delicate paper cuts or to wonder at the way in which workers create their own designs and cut the paper by hand. In the same factory we saw the famous Chinese kites and lanterns being made in all manner of shapes and sizes.

One thinks of painting as a very individual art. I therefore found it difficult to accept the term "art factory," but it is a definite industry in China. Artists are employed to produce their own paintings or make copies of ancient scenes from tombs and temples, and it seems there is a constant demand for these works. Art scrolls hang in most homes, and good reproductions of ancient art or original compositions particularly of mountains, flowers and animals, find a ready market. Streets are lined, often for blocks, with stalls featuring paintings and scrolls which seem to be in constant demand.

Art is part of every child's training, and is inherent in Chinese culture. Chinese children's art exhibits are famous and have travelled world wide. I have hanging in my living room, a thirty- by twenty-inch painting of birds and trees produced by a four-year-old boy whose work ranks with a mature adult's painting. I watched the little lad paint the picture as his father, also a painter, stood by. He told us the boy had begun to paint at two years of age, and I thought of my two-year-old granddaughter crayonning wild designs in her scribbler.

As the standard of living in China is steadily rising and the overseas demand for her goods increases, the pressure on Chinese industry is enormous. The need for new equipment and modern technology creates problems because of the need for hard currency to purchase abroad. Rampant pollution and resource depletion add to critical concern for the future.

The state is stepping up efforts to promote the integration of industry and scientific research centres in an attempt to speed up development and production. In February 1987, the State Economic Commission announced a move to encourage business and science institutes to form united enterprises to develop new and better products. At the same time, new shipping lines are being opened, and a large ocean-going fleet, now the seventh largest in the world, is to be expanded to handle increased foreign trade.

"Raise Your Standards" was the ultimatum to China's light industry delivered to a conference in January, 1987. Two major tasks were outlined: to produce more refined goods, and to re-orient production to overseas markets.

On a different, but very significant plane, is the revival of the Gung Ho Industrial Cooperatives. Nurtured and developed during the War of Resistance against Japan by the indomitable New Zealander, Rewi Alley, they were a vital element in harnessing the productive capacities of the millions of refugees from Japanese aggression.

In 1937, Rewi Alley was chief factory inspector for the Municipal Council of the International Settlement in Shanghai. Together with Edgar and Peg Snow and other supporters both foreign and Chinese, he organized unemployed and refugee workers. In 1938, the Association for the Advancement of Chinese Industrial Cooperatives was set up in Wuhan, with Rewi Alley as technical advisor. In less than four years, over 2,000 co-ops began supplying the resistance forces with much needed supplies. In addition, they produced goods to meet the needs of the populace displaced by the advancing Japanese armies.

Reverend Hall, the Anglican Bishop of Hong Kong, headed up an international committee to support the cooperatives. Over ten million American dollars flowed into China from all over the world. The term "Gung Ho" became a familiar expression in English to express whole-hearted support for a worthy cause.

Travelling continually to establish co-ops, Rewi Alley saw the need for trained organizers. In the early forties, he set up a technical training school in Shandan, in the north-west province of Gansu. The students were able to spread the idea of collective ownership by members who democratically elected officers to manage the enterprise. Millions of bolts of cloth, blankets, weapons and ammunition were manufactured by refugees who became self-supporting through their participation in the co-ops.

Unfortunately, the Kuomintang Government, resenting the success of the co-ops, was anything but supportive. They attempted to take over the enterprises to gain the profits for themselves. Organizers were jailed, beaten, tortured or even buried alive. But in spite of war and opposition, the co-ops persisted, often moving back into the hills to escape political interference or enemy forces.

After civil war was resolved and the People's Republic set up, co-ops became less important. People were resettled, given land and eventually become members of the commune system or industrial unions. Recently, however, the feeling has grown that "Gung Ho" cooperatives are not outdated. Rewi Alley (in his eighties, but still active) became concerned about growing unemployment among the youth, as mechanization freed many labourers and the baby boom of the fifties and sixties poured millions of workers into the labour force. The training of co-op organizers has been re-activated and pilot projects established in several centres.

The new impetus was apparent at a cooperative conference convened in Wuhan in November 1989. Spurred on by the memory of Rewi Alley, whose death in Beijing in 1988 was mourned by the Chinese people, the delegates were determined to carry on his work. George LeBeau, of White Rock, British Columbia, who was in China as part of the Canadian delegation attending the Bethune Commemorative Celebrations, joined the International Committee of Gung Ho Co-ops to attend the conference.

George said, "When we arrived at the Honglin Experimental Cooperative Village for opening exercises, we were escorted by four teenaged girls dressed in beautiful red and black uniforms. Flanked by school children in uniform, their school band of bugles and drums and hundreds of flags, we marched down the street to the hall where opening ceremonies were held to honour the memory and spirit of Rewi Alley."

After tributes to the untiring energies of Alley, George LeBeau and the other delegates visited a 1,600-member village co-op, complete with spacious and comfortable two-storey homes. They also visited textile, weaving and garment co-op factories. The next day, agricultural, fishing and wine co-ops welcomed the visitors, and they were given the opportunity to see a factory producing parkas for the Soviet Union. Most impressive was the Garment and Handicrafts Co-op operated by handicapped people producing excellent shellwork, embroidered slippers and work clothing. Plans are in the works for the organization of further co-ops for the handicapped throughout the country.

Representatives present from overseas co-ops were eager to encourage a system of international cooperative trading. With the revived International Committee offering some financial support and leadership in organization, educational programs and marketing techniques, the enthusiasm and determination of the Gung Ho movement should pay great dividends.

In the recently published booklet "Rewi Alley On Gung Ho," Alley writes:

> The youth of China left unemployed can become a menace to society. Fully and creatively organised, they can be a source of enormous additional strength. I hope that now, from its very small and simple beginnings, the Gung Ho rebirth will catch the imagination of many, so that they will join it and find full expression for their own creativeness.

China's industry, be it controlled by the state, the township or cooperatives, is on the march. With the opening up of the country's rich natural resources and the demand for consumer goods, the potential for development is enormous.

But international reaction to the events in Tiananmen Square has seriously affected the economy of China. Loans have been refused, joint ventures have been terminated and the once buoyant tourist industry has been radically curtailed. Corruption and mismanagement have also taken their toll. A restless business class could add fuel to the current dissidence. Much more careful planning and cooperation on the part of the government is essential to the resolution of China's present dilemma.

23. The Women of China

Women in China, like women everywhere, are on the move. Mao's dictum that "women hold up half the sky," laid the foundation for a revolutionary approach to freeing women from their oppression and isolation.

Confucian philosophy for centuries had laid heavy restraints on women. They were always under the authority of a male: father, brother, husband or son. At marriage a woman became not only subservient to her husband but often a slave in her in-laws' home. Her cultural standards were low and she was haunted by an overwhelming sense of inferiority.

This feeling of inferiority was imposed on her as part of a social code which grew basically out of the Chinese philosophy of Yin and Yang. Yin represented the dark, weak, passive, so-called female attributes; yang represented the bright, strong, active male attributes. Both were essential to life and served to balance each other. Male philosophers, therefore, dictated that women must be, of necessity, passive and obedient to men.

To help maintain this obedience there developed a vicious custom of foot binding, which originated in the tenth century towards the end of the T'ang dynasty. According to early records, a beautiful concubine dancing on a six-foot-high golden lotus was commanded by the emperor to bind her feet with white silk cloth to make her feet look like moon points. There is no evidence that this binding was restrictive, but it became fashionable for women to bind their feet as a sign of gentility and refinement. By the end of the twelfth century, the custom was accepted throughout the imperial palace.

Men encouraged this custom and demanded that the feet, known as the "golden lotus" be as small as possible. This, they said, distinguished women from men, and more importantly, it restricted women's ability to walk about. They were confined to their quarters, unable to "wander about as lewdly as they pleased." The restriction guaranteed their chastity and became a symbol of male dominance.

The custom then took on sexual overtones. The small feet and tiny steps caused the body to sway and the hips to undulate which further attracted males. The 2½ to 3-inch shoe suggested concealment and the secrecy of the boudoir where the foot was washed and bound. Lovers stroked and fondled it, and women made elegant embroidered red silk shoes to wear to bed to contrast with their fair skin and make them even more desirable.

When the Manchus came to power in 1644, their Mongolian background of a carefree life on the open steppes rebelled at the habit of foot binding. The practice was decried. So entrenched had the custom become, however, that it persisted into the twentieth century. I own two embroidered women's shoes, one 2½ inches long, the other 3¼ inches, given to my Mother by two women who had gone through the painful process of unbinding their feet. Little old ladies with very small feet can still be seen, obviously victims of childhood foot binding.

From earliest times, women suffered under the yoke of a feudal marriage system. Girls were usually betrothed in childhood by their parents, who received money and betrothal gifts. At marriageable age, the girl would move to live with her husband's family under the control of her mother-in-law, severing all connections with her own family. In an upper-class family she would probably see second and third wives or concubines added to the household, particularly if she failed to produce a male heir. She could be divorced by her husband at will. Remarriage was out of the question as she was an object of scorn and contempt. If her husband died she was required to wear widow's weeds for the rest of her life. As she had no economic independence, life was bitter unless — as was rarely the case — she was fortunate enough to marry into an unusually caring family.

A woman was not permitted to marry a second time or take part in sacrificial ceremonies. Stories of the experiences of women are endless. A seventeen-year-old bride-to-be hanged herself when her betrothed died; another married her fiance's memorial tablet when he died, and she never left the courtyard for the remainder of her life.

Over the door of a home in Qufu hangs a tablet presented by the emperor which bears the inscription: "To a family replete with loyalty and filial piety." When the head of the household was defeated in battle and committed suicide, the son killed himself, and the wife hanged herself as a symbol of her chastity and devotion.

Old Chinese sayings ran: "Noodles are not rice and women are not human beings," or "A wife is like a pony. I'll ride her and whip her as I like."

Although women were beginning to gain a small measure of freedom by the beginning of the twentieth century, the power of the family was still very strong. I can remember in 1937, one of my former students coming to me in tears. Her mother had died and she was the eldest of the family. Her father was insisting that she must marry to create a home for her brothers and sisters. Although her father had lived for several years in Australia and she herself was largely schooled there, the old ideas persisted. Her father and aunts had picked a man for her, and family pressure was brought to bear on her. She herself was a Christian and the man was not, although he had agreed to study the Christian faith.

"What if I fall in love with someone else later on?" she said. "I don't love this man."

I offered her asylum but her sense of responsibility for her brothers and sisters finally prevailed, and she submitted to the marriage. I corresponded with her for a time, but because of the war we lost contact. I have often wondered how her life has been.

In the revolutionary struggle of the 1940s, women found a place for themselves. Six months before Liberation was achieved, the first National Congress of Women was held in March 1949. Anticipating the success of the Communist Revolution, the women of the already liberated areas decided it was time to establish a nation-wide women's organization. Accordingly, on April 3, 1949 in Beijing, six months before the People's Republic was proclaimed, the All-China Democratic Women's Federation was founded. Their goals were:

> to unite Chinese women of all nationalities and democratic classes so that they can exert their united strength to work in various fields of national construction, to protect women's rights and interests, to promote child welfare, to ensure equality of women, and to rally all peace-loving women the world over in defence of peace.

Membership in the Federation was by affiliated groups organized at the local, county, provincial and national level. The groups were organized in schools, factories, residential communities and wherever women were located. Study groups introduced them to socialist ideals, economic conditions and women's rights and dealt with practical and emotional problems faced by the emergence of women in the marketplace and in the social and political arena. Centuries of suppression and indoctrination of inferiority made the emancipation of women a heavy task.

Hand in hand with the freeing of women from the chains of the past was the emphasis on improvement in the welfare of children. Hygiene for mother and child, nurseries, midwifery classes, the training of good teachers, doctors, nursery supervisors and economic workers were part of the program for reconstructing the new society.

In Shanghai, I talked to several women who gave me some insights into their lives. "I'm a cigarette factory worker," one woman explained. "At twelve I began working in a factory. We girl labourers did the same work as adults and we worked thirteen hours a day. I lived in a six-by-seven-metre room and had a long walk to the factory every day."

She looked like an eighteen-year-old school girl but I discovered she was forty-two and had thirty years of working experience. I asked her if she was married.

"Yes, I have a girl of fifteen and a boy of seventeen and they are studying in school, such a happy childhood compared to mine. When they were smaller, I brought them to the factory where we had a nursery and kindergarten. And now I have a subsidy so that I can take public transportation to my work."

The area I was visiting was formerly a red-light district and as another woman, Mrs. Wu told me her story in picturesque language, I wondered if she had been a victim of the vicious system of prostitution.

"I lived opposite the number one department store on one of the 'vanity streets' of Shanghai," Mrs. Wu began. "Before Liberation the area was covered with a pestilential atmosphere and was populated by gangsters, gamblers and one hundred and one prostitutes. From six in the evening the area was 'bitter'. There were twenty-four brothels with lamps at the front gate. The names of the prostitutes were written there to attract rich clients. Prostitutes also roamed the streets with painted faces to entice customers. One brothel boss, whose title was Number 774, was nicknamed 'Pock Face.' He exploited the girls who came mostly from rural areas."

"Why did they come to work for him?" I asked.

"Their parents were destitute and they sold their daughters to him. If a girl refused to meet a guest she was punished, usually by flogging. Eventually many of them suffered serious illnesses and were often then tortured to death. Pock Face even tried to force his own beautiful nineteen-year-old daughter to be a prostitute. When she refused, he threatened to turn her out of her home. It was impossible for a single girl to live on her own, so she committed suicide.

"The brothels were licensed by the Kuomintang government. Many of them were owned by officials, and it was impossible for the girls to do anything to protect themselves. The government was so corrupt, the saying was, 'if you're arrested at the front door of the police station, you're released at the back door.'

"After Liberation, the brothels were immediately prohibited. Some owners surrendered their licences, but some stubbornly refused and went underground. Finally in 1952, strict measures were taken to tighten controls, and owners were tracked down by local citizens, tried and convicted. Pock Face was given fifteen years in jail and then was sent to a rural area to do physical labour in a commune. Finally he reformed himself.

"The prostitutes were not considered to blame for their lives. They were first sent to hospitals for medical treatment and then given an education because they ranged in age from ten to about thirty years of age. After several years of training they were given the choice of returning to their home villages or being assigned jobs in the city."

When Mrs. Wu finished with all her information, a very determined little lady who had been waiting anxiously to tell me her story, came forward. "I was a drug addict," she said. "During my first pregnancy my health was not good so my husband, who took drugs, urged me to take some. He was working in a bank, but eventually lost his job and finally died of addiction. By this time I had become addicted too, and I sold my seven-year-old son for drug money. When he died later of measles I had no interest other than drugs. But I couldn't give up my bad habit. My goods were all in the pawn shop and I knew that I would soon die in the gutter."

"But you didn't," I commented. "What saved you?"

"After Liberation there was an anti-drug campaign. Teams of workers talked to me and at last I made up my mind to try to break the habit. I didn't want to go to hospital so I lay on my bed, and for three days and nights I never slept, but just lay staring at the ceiling, screaming and crying, or pacing the floor. But the team stood by me. After three days the worst was over. Eventually I was able to join the 'ban addiction' group and I began telling people of my personal sufferings and helping them to conquer the habit. Now I'm referred to as a 'ghost turned into a human being'."

She was certainly a vigorous ghost and an active member of her local production team. She had married a worker in a chemical light industry plant and had a daughter who worked in a bank and a son-in-law in the army. "Liberation" had special significance for her.

My favourite story to come out of my contacts with women in new China was that of Han Ji Shun. In 1958, at the age of forty-eight, she had gone to night school to learn to read. Eight years later, still active and enterprising, and with her eight children grown up, she announced that she intended to go to work for the Revolution. Her husband violently objected. Their income was more than adequate, he contended, and she was too old to face the difficulties of work in industry.

But Han Ji Shun wasn't concerned about money; she simply wanted to repay her country for what it had done for women and for society.

"Look," she said to me as she rolled up her pant leg. "In the old society I was apprenticed at twelve years of age in a cigarette factory. These are the scars from beatings I received. My wages were ten cents a day and I hadn't enough to eat or wear. Now children can go to school and women are liberated. I must do my share."

Mrs. Han's husband finally agreed to study Chairman Mao's works with his wife. In the end, he allowed her to put their savings into an industry if something suitable could be found.

Meanwhile, with eight other housewives with no technical or organizational experience, Han Ji Shun had been searching for an innovative project to which they could turn their energies.

"We have two hands," they said. "We cannot stay home and remain idle. It is time to leave our stoves and step over the threshold."

They began looking for waste material that they could turn to productive use. All the while their husbands scoffed.

"Run a noodle factory," they said. "If you women get into difficulty, you will cry and blow your noses."

The comments merely served to strengthen the women's determination. Indignantly they said, "what men can do, we can do."

They discovered that steel shavings and rusted iron could be processed, powdered and pressed into items. They set to work to plan a factory and give the lie to those who opposed them. With nothing but borrowed shovels and their bare hands they began to build a kiln. They collected broken fire bricks from factories and built the inside of the kiln with them, constructing the outside with common red bricks.

Since the cost of 30,000 yuan for a chimney was out of the question, they went off and learned to weld. Then, getting old oil barrels from some of the factories, they rolled them down the street to the field where they were working. Removing the ends, they welded them together and made a chimney which still stands today outside the museum shed showing their first crude tools and equipment. Borrowing a winch and ropes from a bridge beam factory they put up their chimney.

The next problem was obtaining the buildings. Refusing to ask for money from the state, they built earth adobe huts. The roofs were so low that a tall man could touch the ceiling, but the women were proud to work in them.

By now the community was beginning to take an interest. Workers from a nearby factory helped them build a bake house, and other structures were put around the workers while production was proceeding. Husbands began to offer assistance and technical advice; even the children became involved. Thus was born the Chun Gung Metallurgical Powder Products Neighbourhood Factory.

At first all operations were manual, resulting in slow and inefficient procedures. "It was pleasant," laughed Mrs. Han, "because there was no noise, but we had to have modern equipment. We wouldn't stretch out our hands for money, but we went to the factories to study their techniques."

The women began by washing oxidized iron to get rid of the oil, earth and sand attached. They learned a magnetic process that drew out the iron, but it took twenty people fifteen days to fill the kiln using hand magnetizers. They then developed a magnetic dressing machine which filled the kiln in a day. Metal cases of pure oxidized iron were then fired in the kiln and the resulting cakes crushed into metallurgical powder. With the addition of other materials and further firing at intense heat, the powder was made into rings, tubes, bushings, bearings, scale weights — over two hundred items. Soon demand exceeded supply. Large factories began bringing their designs to the women to turn out the parts they required. The number of workers grew to 229, of which 168 were women.

When I first met Mrs. Han, she was sixty-six and had just stepped down from the chairpersonship of the factory. Along with one other of the original nine women, she was now working as vice-chairperson in support of the young woman who had assumed the overall responsibilities. She had seen a grass field become a well-housed 2000-square-metre factory with a tall brick chimney and mechanization, a manual operation turn into an industry with fifty pieces of equipment and an earth kiln replaced by an electric oven.

"We fall short of demand," said Mrs. Han. "We're not mechanized enough, we don't produce the variety of products we should and we cannot produce the more complicated items yet. But we are improving. Other small factories like ours have been encouraged to start up around our city of Shenyang."

I took Mrs. Han's picture with the young woman who had stepped into her shoes, and tried inadequately to express my admiration for the astounding achievement of this little woman who said she intended to keep working for another four years until she was seventy.

"My husband is retired now," she concluded, "so he gets the meals ready. I have good health so I'll continue to work for the Revolution."

Many women like Mrs. Han, with their initiative and drive, have sparked innovative developments and given leadership in their communities. But changes in attitude come slowly. It amazed me when I was teaching in Yantai University in 1986, to hear a male student say he longed for the day when it wouldn't be necessary for women to work so they could stay home, like most Japanese women, and look after their husbands.

In fairness to Chinese men, this attitude was not widely supported by his fellow students, and it is certainly not the policy of the government. However, women are still not represented in the high offices of the state, and they are fighting an uphill battle to achieve recognition and positions of prominence. As the first secretary of the Women's Federation at the 1986 National Congress said, as quoted in the *China Daily*, "millions upon millions of drops of water make a river and the impact of our concerted efforts is beyond measure." The new constitution, adopted by the Federation at its 1986 Congress, invited applications for membership from all national and local women's organizations — including the YWCA and women's work committees from industry, commerce and agriculture — in order to strengthen the struggle for equality.

Much has been made in the Western press of female babies being left to die since families can have only one child and the preference is for a male. Undoubtedly this has happened in a limited number of cases, but the government does not tolerate such acts, and punishment has been swift. The desire for a male child, however, is still very strong, particularly in the countryside, and the new responsibility system encourages this obsession. With so much farm work still done manually, peasant families feel the need for male workers to increase productivity and income. The price of the new responsibility system is high.

One woman told me, "It is sad sometimes to see the look on the father's face when the nurse says 'it's a girl'."

There is, however, a changing attitude. "Parents in the thirty- to forty-year-old range," one young Chinese woman commented, "tend to put much more emphasis on a boy than those under thirty, and city dwellers are much less concerned."

I recently discussed with a young woman in her late twenties some of the problems of women in China. She herself came from a middle class family. Her parents had had some education, and when Liberation came, they were able to upgrade their standards by attending university and were then able to secure good jobs. Consequently, she and her brother were brought up in an enlightened home where there was no discrimination whatsoever between the two children. Both were encouraged to attend university. But to qualify for the limited openings at the university level meant unceasing study and little opportunity for social activity or leisure time.

"In the city," she commented, "ordinary women enjoy equality, and subservience is not a major factor because women have an independent income. In the countryside men and women work side by side and share responsibilities. But women still bear more of the responsibility of the home. Intellectual young women want to be successful in business but they also want to be good mothers and wives. Factory women, I don't think, are so concerned with success in their work. Their aim is first of all to be a good mother, secondly a good wife and thirdly, to be a good worker." It was an interesting assessment by a university graduate born and bred in the city.

From several highly educated women, however, I have heard a common complaint. One woman expressed it. "It's very hard to find a husband," she said. "We women want a man with the same or better education, whereas the men are satisfied with someone with less education."

"Why must your husband have an equal education?" I asked.

"If I have a Ph.D. and my husband has only an M.A., when he is forced to do housework he will complain that I consider myself better than he."

It was a telling commentary on an attitude that is perhaps not unique in China. "There's too much pressure on getting married," the young woman claimed. "Single women are still not acceptable."

"And if a woman is not married," added another, "she must stay with her parents. Because of the housing shortage, no accommodation is available to single people. Even when there is a space, single persons are passed over. The policy of the government of 'no marriage, no need for a house' puts pressure on us to marry."

"It isn't just the government," cut in one of the other women. "Society forces us to marry. People don't approve of us remaining single."

Said a thirty-five-year-old single woman unhappily, "Those of us who were sent to the countryside during the Cultural Revolution and then came back to our studies were older than the new students. The men who came back tended to marry younger women or decided to remain single to devote their energies to their new careers."

These comments were certainly supported in a commentary in the *China Daily* in February 1987. An article entitled "Show More Concern for Singles" highlights the very issues these women had detailed. It stressed the point that the country was facing a situation where conventional approaches to marriage were clashing with modern notions, which was leading to a break with traditional and parental ideas.

According to Chinese tradition, the basic unit of Chinese society is the family, not the individual. An unmarried person is "abnormal" and is subject to prejudice and loneliness. Yet in Beijing alone it is estimated there are about 150,000 lonely singles, the majority of them women. Multiplied by the hundreds of cities in China, the number must be enormous. Chinese society has not come to grips with this new phenomenon, and "singles" are misunderstood by society in general.

No comment on the women of China would be complete without reference to Madame Soong Ching-ling, wife of Dr. Sun Yat-sen. She is the sister of Madame Chiang Kai-shek (Soong May-ling) and Madame H. H. Kung (Soong Ai-ling), but elected to throw in her lot with the Revolutionary forces. She became a powerful and moving force on behalf of the women and children of China and used her honoured place in China to this end.

I was indeed proud of the University of Victoria, in British Columbia, Canada, when in 1981 its president, Dr. Howard Petch, and some of the university staff journeyed to Beijing to bestow an honourary degree on Madame Soong. Her death shortly afterwards was deeply mourned. Her memory is still very much alive because of her tenacious struggle on behalf of the women and children of her beloved country.

"The women's liberation movement," she said in 1971, "will be ended when and only when the process of the social transformation of society as a whole is completed."

Mao's call to women to "hold up half the sky," and the public-spirited and selfless work of countless dedicated women have freed Chinese women from the bondage of the past. But much still remains to be done.

24. Religions of China

"Not another temple," groaned the group.

"But this is a very special one," explained the guide. "This one dates from the T'ang dynasty and it was built by the Emperor in A.D. 785."

"They're all special," said a sceptical tourist.

But to each guide, his or her temple *is* special, and it is necessary to appreciate the central place that temples have in the life and culture of China.

"How many temples are there in this country?" someone wanted to know. I doubt if anyone has ever counted them. They dot the Chinese landscape on mountains veiled in mist, stand on the river banks challenging floods or are hidden behind walls in the centre of cities. They stand as age-old structures to honour Lao-tse, Confucius, Buddha or any deity or venerated personage worthy of commemoration.

Evidence of observances with some religious significance date back to antiquity. Bronze vessels from the Shang dynasty in 1700 B.C. designed for use in burial and ancestor worship, have been discovered in the ancient capital of Anyang. China has only produced one indigenous religion — Taoism. Confucianism was a philosophy that developed rituals of veneration of ancestors and ceremonies, based on the moral role of man in society. Buddhism, Islamism and Christianity were imported from outside.

Lao-tse, from whose brief writings Taoism evolved, was a contemporary of Confucius and lived in the sixth century B.C. He proclaimed that there was a harmony between earth and heaven, that the same laws governed both, and, if man simply learned to appreciate and work with whatever happened, the end result would be a serene and happy state. This cooperation between heaven and earth, between man and nature, he called Tao — the Way.

"God created heaven and earth by his Tao," said Lao-tse. "Tao is the origin of the Universe. All things come from Tao."

Many of his teachings parallel the words of Jesus: "For the gentle and weak shall overcome the powerful and strong," "He who wants to be great let him first humble himself," and " The saint does not accumulate for himself. The more he lives for others the richer his wealth abounds."

Like Paul the Apostle, Lao-tse chose three virtues. "Three things I cherish most: the first is love, the second is self-denial, the third is never to be the first in the world. For love is victorious in battle, invulnerable in defense. Heaven arms with love those on whom it would bestow salvation."

Lao-tse admitted that his sayings were easy to understand, but the world did not understand or practise them. He did not establish an organized religion, but a monk who followed his way built a monastery where Lao Tse's disciples could study and worship.

I was privileged in 1988, to visit and stay overnight in this monastery in the mountains some distance from the city of Chengdu. It is an active centre of worship in a beautiful setting, visited daily by many pilgrims.

Taoism, being more mystical and, therefore, more difficult for people to grasp than the rituals and sacrifices of Confucianism, did develop over the centuries philosophical, monastic and folk religious forms which have survived over the centuries.

Serenity is one of the most noticeable characteristics of a true Taoist. I saw this in the person of a dear old man who was head of the Taoist temple in the city of Chengdu. Although 103 years old, he was alert and ready to receive our group most graciously.

Occasionally, we saw Taoist priests in their black caps and cloaks and their tight leggings on the streets of China. Professor Joseph Needham, the eminent Cambridge scholar, claims that Taoism, as such, is on the decline, but the basic philosophy of the harmony of opposites is relevant to the nuclear age and is the philosophy of the future.

Confucius, a contemporary of Lao-tse, did not found a religion. Confucianism is an involved system to maintain social order. The feudal system of Confucius' time was breaking down; disorder, corruption and chaos were prevalent. His concern was to restore order by building high moral standards. If moral harmony could be established, he contended that political harmony would result. If men knew what was wrong and the evil it caused, they would avoid it. To find the best in human nature and steadfastly to cultivate it, was practically the essence of Confucian ethics. In order to establish the social order that he envisaged, rites for family worship and for public celebrations were drawn up. Sacrifices to heaven, to ancestors and to the spirits of earth were meant to create in the worshipper a respectful state of mind which would regulate his conduct and, ipso facto, the conduct of the nation and the world.

As a political system aimed at the restoration of a feudal order, Confucianism is totally out of date. But, as a code for the conduct of society, it has probably something to offer. A political order based on moral order, and political and social harmony achieved by moral harmony in man himself with a strong sense of responsibility towards one's fellow beings has something to contribute to a nation today.

It is probably with this in mind that interest in Confucianism has been revived in China. In September 1986, on the occasion of Confucius' birthday, elaborate memorial services were held in Qufu, the city of his birth. With the solemn music of drums and bells, a long procession of richly dressed ceremonial attendants assembled before the Confucian temples where sacrificial offerings were made. The Qufu Opera troupe performed the traditional dances, accompanied by an orchestra of ancient instruments. It was an almost unbelievable performance in a Communist society.

The city of Qufu is unique. Since the Cultural Revolution, it has been transformed from a small provincial town to a tourist centre. Tourism has, so far at least, not spoiled the atmosphere of the place. I felt, as I wandered about the city in 1986, as if I had gone back in time. The spirit of Confucius seemed to hover over the temple, which is one of the three oldest, grandest and best preserved buildings in China.

The temple complex covered more than twenty hectares and had nine courtyard. It was first built in 478 B.C., rebuilt on several occasions, reaching its present size in the fifteenth and sixteenth centuries. I found the names of gates and archways intriguing, especially the "Arch of the Sound of Metal and the Vibration of Jade." This phrase, used in an ancient book to describe the complete process of a musical performance, symbolized the epitome of Confucian philosophy. The "Arch of the Spirit of the Universe" and the "Arch of Virtue Equal to Heaven and Earth," indicating Confucian doctrine, led into various courtyards. Streams and bridges, gates and huge carved stone tablets enticed me on, until I reached the thirteen tablet pavilions. These magnificent red plaster and ornate gold-tiled buildings housed over fifty stone tablets which recorded Confucian doctrine and the history of the reconstruction of the Temple. Nearby was the Apricot Terrace whose fruit trees were planted when the structure was built in 1017 over the place where Confucius gave lectures to his disciples.

The main edifice in the temple complex was the superb Dacheng Hall with its striking carved stone columns. On each of the ten pillars two dragons playing with a pearl were carved in deep relief, treasures of sculptural art.

A beautiful hotel had just been built in Qufu, although wisely, it was executed in the traditional Chinese style. But I was glad that I was able to stay in one section of the Confucius family mansion, where Confucius' descendants have lived for the past several hundred years. Some of the rooms were still furnished in the traditional style; others had been somewhat modernized for guests. Wandering through the courtyards to the dining room, or passing through the gateways to the bustling street, I sensed the ghosts of the past.

It was as I walked through the pathways of the cemetery, however, that time seemed to stand still. Here, in the enormous two-hundred-hectare park, were buried all seventy-six generations of Confucius' family since his death in 479 B.C., the world's longest ancestral line. The quiet solitude, the singing of birds and the unobtrusive tablets that marked the graves hidden in natural growth, created an almost eerie atmosphere. Something of the spirit of moral harmony which he preached seemed to linger in the "Sage's Forest."

In Qufu, as in every other city and town of China, there are also Buddhist temples. In the past few years, I have visited fifty cities and towns in the course of my travels in China and I am sure I have been in nearly as many temples.

Buddhism originated in India with the teaching of Sakyamuni, later known as Buddha, who lived from 563 - 480 B.C., and the religion spread to China around A.D. 220. It was the first foreign religion successfully transplanted into China, brought by a monk, whose journey to India to bring back the scriptures, is recorded in the famous Chinese classic *Journey to the West*.

The centre of Buddhist life was the monastery. Retreating from the problems of everyday life, men and women settled usually on a beautiful mountain or in a rural setting where nature provided inspiration. So popular did the religion become that, during the Sung dynasty (A.D. 960-1127), there were three million monks in northern China alone, which had a total population of sixty million. Chinese monks did not beg but lived off the income from lands donated by the rich. As a result they eventually became part of the hated landlord system. They contributed greatly to Chinese life, however. Monasteries were open to travellers, and hospitality was freely offered. Monks and nuns often acted as social service agencies.

Buddhism also inspired a very high level of architecture and sculpture, enriching enormously the cultural life of China. Statues of Buddha are everywhere. Near Jinan I visited the Hill of the Thousand Buddhas. Figures of all sizes, from a few inches to several feet, were to be found in niches and caves covering the hillside near a well-kept cemetery associated with a once-famous Buddhist monastery. At Leshan in Szechuan province I viewed an enormous Buddha carved out of a whole mountain, his big toe nail alone so large that a picnic party was sitting on it having lunch. In Huhhot in Inner Mongolia, the Five Pagoda Temple is totally covered with thousands of small carvings of Buddha. In Menghai on the border of Thailand, I visited a Buddhist school for boys training to be monks, their temple a straw thatched wooden structure with carved Buddhist statues.

One of the most fascinating centres of Buddhist art and sculpture is in Dunhuang. On my journey along the ancient Silk Road, I stopped where the silk caravans of the middle ages paused to worship before beginning the arduous and dangerous trek across the desert and the snow-capped mountains with their silks and spices for Europe. From the fifth to the ninth century A.D., religious patrons of the arts sent eminent artists and sculptors to Dunhuang to paint and carve Buddhas and religious scenes in the four-hundred-odd caves in the hills. Because of the very dry climate these works of art have been preserved intact.

From the mid-nineteenth century to the mid-twentieth, Buddhism became excessively corrupt and monasteries were often centres of degeneracy, slavery and manipulation. When the monasteries lost their lands with redistribution in 1949, and reactionary secret societies were dissolved, faithful followers used the opportunity to reform and purify their religion. In May 1953, the Association of Chinese Buddhists was founded, bringing together different sects, nationalities and orders who established basic principles of cleansing, compassion and service. Because life is now secure in China, only the dedicated and faithful are seeking ordination, and Buddhism has actually become stronger. All over China I saw the revival of Buddhism. Temples have been redecorated, young monks are in training and worshippers are in evidence.

An ancient Chinese scroll has a rather interesting commentary on the beliefs of Taosim, Confucianism and Buddhism. The painting is entitled "The Vinegar Tasters." Around the vat of vinegar stand three characters representing Confucius, Buddha and Lao-tse. Each has dipped his finger in the vinegar and the reaction to the taste is etched in their faces. Confucius displays a sour look, Buddha a bitter, and Lao-tse is smiling. In this allegorical painting the great teachers dip into Chi, the essence of life. Confucius is distressed by the disorder of public and private life; to Buddha life is full of suffering and bitterness and to escape is man's chief goal. But to Lao-tse, the harmony between heaven and earth is open to anyone, bringing peace and happiness.

The next foreign religion to gain a foothold in China was Islam. In the sixth century A.D., the Turks extended their influence into Asia through the Mongolian tribes who had come into conflict with Muslim power. Today the people of China's west and northwest are predominantly Muslim, with the Grand Mosque of China located in Xian, the starting point of the Silk Road leading to Asia Minor and Europe. I visited an attractive mosque in Huhhot in Inner Mongolia, a mosque and a beautiful sandstone minaret in the desert near Turpan and a fine Muslim hospital in Urumqi.

Christianity was a latecomer to China. During the T'ang dynasty (A.D.618 - 877), which was the golden age of Chinese culture, the imperial house was receptive to foreign influence. Although they had supreme confidence in their own cultural heritage, they were not averse to borrowing outside art forms and faiths. When Nestorian Christians arrived from Persia in 635, they won the support of the emperor, but with the fall of the dynasty and the opposition of Taoists and Buddhists, Nestorian Christianity was nearly wiped out. It was revived again, however, under the Mongols and by 1300 there were seventy-two Nestorian monasteries in China.

About this time Jesuit missionaries arrived, and by the sixteenth century there was a flowering of Christian missions in the Orient. But with the arrival of Franciscan and Dominican priests, who condemned the Jesuit liberal policy of accommodating Christian beliefs to local customs, reconciliation became impossible. By the beginning of the eighteenth century, Christianity practically died out in China. It was not until 1807, when the Protestant Robert Morrison arrived in Macao, that the missionary movement was revived. His mastery of the Chinese language made possible the translation of the Bible, and in 1814, the first Chinese Protestant convert was baptized. Morrison, however, was not allowed to enter the country. Anti-foreign sentiment was widespread in the nineteenth century, and Christianity became a symbol of foreign intrusion. Nevertheless, in spite of critical and often hostile attitudes, Christian missions in China grew at a phenomenal rate until the Second World War.

With the success of the Communists in 1949, missionaries, along with nearly all foreigners, were asked to leave the country. The Chinese church carried on, graduating some ministers, but when the Cultural Revolution took over in 1966, churches and temples were closed for ten years and Christians were often persecuted. In 1974, I visited the staff of Nanjing Theological College and found a college in limbo. The students were in the countryside, and the staff were marking time. Little had changed in 1976, but when I returned in the 1980s, the picture was completely different.

With the overthrow of the Gang of Four in late 1976, tension was eased and the New Constitution in 1978 guaranteed freedom of religion. Churches were gradually restored to the Christians, sometimes with back payment of rent for the period of their occupation. Temples were permitted to reopen, and a new period of religious witness was ushered in.

Before long, 1,600 Christian churches had been re-opened. An average of three new congregations are being formed each week. The demand for pastors and leaders is so critical that short six-week to six-month courses and correspondence courses are being offered, and a number of new theological colleges have been established. Chinese Protestants are more united than ever in history. They have entered what they call the "post-denominational era," and they number three times as many professing Christians as in 1949.

All Protestants are united under the China Christian Council and the National Three-Self Patriotic Movement Committee. The Council's responsibilities entail: strengthening pastoral care, printing and distributing Bibles, the new hymn book and religious journals and books, establishing theological colleges and offering short-term courses.

Closely allied with the Council is the National Three-Self Movement which has adopted the three principles of self-government, self-support, and self-propagation. At this time the church in China does want to be a part of the world-wide ecumenical movement. The organization welcomes cooperation, but on their own terms: "We want to be part of the universal church," they say, "not just a dot on the missionary map of the Western churches."

"The fourth commandment is to honour one's parents," said a Beijing sales clerk. "The Motherland is to be loved and cherished just like a parent. We are also commanded to love others as we love ourselves," she added, "and that is the spirit of service advocated by our government."

That the church was alive and well was evident to me. I attended services in five different cities and found large churches packed to the doors, sometimes without even standing room. In one case some of the congregation were standing outside the wide open windows taking part in the service. In two cases closed circuit television was set up in the basement for the overflow congregation. Two and three services are held each Sunday beginning as early as 7:00 a.m., and at least one weekday service is held for those who are on Sunday shift work. Because the number of church buildings is inadequate, home churches are common and encourage an intimate fellowship. Classes for those seeking instruction and training are held continually.

The Catholic Church is also experiencing a similar revitalization. Because Rome refused in 1958 to accept bishops elected by the Chinese dioceses, the Catholic Church in China broke from Vatican control and chartered an independent course. Dioceses in China now elect and consecrate their own bishops. I was in the Catholic cathedral in Shanghai at a consecration and the large sanctuary was packed to overflowing long before the service began.

"Why is the church growing so rapidly in China?" I asked. The answers were many and varied. One of the chief reasons is that, since the churches have disassociated themselves from the West and its implied imperialism, Christianity is no longer regarded as a foreign religion, but rather one with which the Chinese people can identify. The "three-self movement" has demonstrated that the church is proudly independent. Foreign intervention would be disastrous.

The traumatic experiences of the Cultural Revolution also affected people. The political system had not satisfied all their needs and there was a craving for religious sustenance. Many also saw in their Christian friends, reliable and conscientious workers and cadres who commanded their respect and offered a tangible influence in their lives.

The opening up of China to Western thought has also further permitted a study of the Christian religion. Many found in it a compatibility with their hopes and dreams of a just and equitable society and were impressed with its elimination of sexual inequality when women's ordination was accepted in the Protestant churches in 1979.

A magazine, *The Bridge — Church Life in China Today*, published bimonthly in English, keeps the world-wide Christian church in touch with their fellow-members in China. It does not hesitate to describe the difficulties as well as the successes, or minimize the problems facing the Christian church, but it is an up-beat account of local struggles and triumphs from local training classes to theological seminaries, and from cottage worship to cathedral services.

Although the Chinese Communists are atheists, only a small percentage of the people are members of the party and subscribe fully to Marxist tenets. Atheism is not propagated, and the party, recognizing the necessity of including all citizens in the task of building a strong, united nation, has written into the Constitution a guarantee of freedom of religious belief and practice and equal treatment for all religions.

25. Of People and Places

One billion people, fifty-six nationalities, 3.7 million square miles of mountains and deserts, lakes and rivers, rolling steppes and lush farmlands — this is China, a country so vast and so complex that no outsider seems capable of understanding what motivates its people or is able to catch the essence of its life. As in any country, the physical characteristics of the countryside itself play a part in shaping its history, the personality of its people and their approach to life.

Many people I have taken to China have expressed surprise at the beauty of the country. Conditioned by pictures of crowded cities and endless rice fields, they are not prepared for the beauty of the mountains, the caves, the river gorges, the white sand coastal beaches, the fantastic terracing and contour farming or even the unusual beauty of sand dunes and occasional desert lakes.

Only about ten percent of China's land mass is arable. Mountain ranges — from the Himalayan foothills in the south-west, to the Tianshan range in the north, the Huangshan mountains of Anhui province, and the extraordinary hills of Guilin — have been a source of artistic inspiration and a religious retreat for centuries. Until one has seen the mist-covered mountains of Huangshan or the Guilin hills, it is difficult to appreciate Chinese art. Painting is not a reproduction of a scene but rather an expression of the feeling, the effect on the artist engendered by the scene.

Celestial Lake near the city of Urumqi in the northwest province of Xinjiang, is truly a heavenly sight. Crescent Lake, curled around the "Singing Sands" of Gansu's desert, is a sudden and unexpected delight. A conquering army, camped at the foot of the sand hills, was covered one night by a standstorm (so the story goes), and the souls of the buried soldiers call continuously from beneath the sand.

The coasts of China are washed by warm currents which make sea bathing a joy. When I spent the summer teaching at Yantai on Bohai Bay, a daily swim was a must, and the packed white sand was the scene of daily student ball games.

It is the rivers, however, that give life to the people of China. Although known as the "sorrow of China," because of its constant flooding and consequent loss of life, the Yellow River in the north sustains millions of people, irrigating the fields, transporting goods, producing fish, creating power and water for daily life. Over the centuries the river devastated the countryside, but now with dikes, China has done much to tame its waywardness.

The third largest river in the world, the Yangtze, flows from the Tibetan plateau to the Pacific, cutting China in two. Once, the hazardous trip through the shoals and rapids took a heavy toll on the trackers who hauled the boats through the teacherous waters, straining at the ropes as they picked their way along the narrow rocky paths on the steep ledges. But blasting and the control of currents has transformed this once perilous journey into a safe and pleasant voyage. A cruise from Chongqing to Wuhan is a favourite trip for visitors. Long flights of steps from the water line to the cities along the banks keep carriers busy. Temples and pagodas perch on high places, offering retreats for the seekers of spiritual peace. Fields terraced along the steep hills testify to the incredible agricultural skills of the farmers. Boats of every size and description ply the waters in a constant stream, ferrying people and goods, serving as a main thoroughfare for a very large precentage of China's inland shipping.

The spectacular beauty of the Three Gorges and the side excursion up the Mini-Gorges never fails to impress the visitor. Once out of the last Gorge, the mighty Gezhou Dam comes into view, providing flood control, irrigation and electric power for central China. Several locks convey ships and barges to the lower reaches of the river which widens out almost to the size of a narrow lake. The scene changes then to fields and towns, as the river flows on to Wuhan and eventually to the huge metropolis of Shanghai.

Four voyages down the Yangtze have not dimmed my appetite for the trip, particularly now that the fine new cruise ships take five days, stopping for side excursions up the Mini-Gorges and day trips to scenic spots and interesting towns.

On the Whampoa River, just before it joins the mouth of the Yangtze, lies Shanghai, the largest city in China with over twelve million inhabitants. Its river harbours hundreds of ships from all corners of the globe as well as the thousands of sampans, tugs, barges, ferries and junks carrying people, animals, and produce to waiting ships, across the river or to the hinterland.

Shanghai is China's leading port, a commercial and manufacturing centre and a major contributor to the financial support of the Chinese economy. Thousands upon thousands of tourists pass through the city every year, visiting the Yu Yuan Gardens set in the midst of old Shanghai, and the Temple of the Jade Buddha famous for its beautiful pale green statue carved from one enormous piece of the precious stone. Visitors walk along the Bund, the river-front promenade once part of the British and French concessions, that offers a never ending panorama of waterfront life.

So numerous and fascinating are the cities of China, that it is impossible to describe them all. But no comment on the notable metropolitan areas could exclude Beijing, China's political, cultural, educational, and historical capital. The Forbidden City, former palace of the Ming and Ch'ing dynasties, the Temple of Heaven where the Emperor worshipped his ancestors and prayed for a good harvest and the Summer Palace, to which the imperial family retired in the heat of the summer are all part of the magic of Beijing. Tiananmen Square surrounded by a gateway retained when the old city wall was torn down, the Mausoleum of Mao Tse-Tung, the Great Hall of the People (the Chinese parliament buildings, the Museum of History and the Forbidden City is the heart of Beijing, and in its centre is the Monument to the People, which memorializes those who gave their lives in the struggle for Liberation. Around the monument's base are carved scenes reminiscent of the century of struggle beginning with the Opium War, followed by the

Taipeng Rebellion, the Boxer Rebellion, the Revolution of 1911, the May Fourth Incident, the struggle with Japan and on the fourth side the celebration of the great victory of the people in 1949.

A description of Beijing would be incomplete without reference to the Great Wall. It runs north of the city extending from the Pacific Ocean to the Gobi Desert, rising and falling, twisting and turning for six thousand kilometres and traversing five provinces. The wall was originally begun by the first emperor of China in 221 B.C., when he joined the walls of the conquered states to form a protective barrier against the marauding northern tribes. During the centuries it was extended, reinforced and rebuilt, and became one of the four great wonders of the world and the only man-made structure visible to the astronauts from the moon. The wall has now no strategic value for defence, but it is preserved as an historical monument. The section most frequently visited lies approximately eighty-five kilometres from Beijing at the Badaling Pass. Another section has now been repaired, however, and I was privileged for the first time to visit this new part in April 1989. So steep is the approach that a cable car has been installed for those who do not want to tackle the steps leading to the top. The view from the summit of the mountains and valleys, the twisting wall and its two-storeyed watch-towers is magnificent.

Fifty kilometres south-west of Beijing is another great historic site. I was able on one occasion to visit Zhoukoudian, where in 1929 was discovered the skull of Peking Man, an ape-like man who lived approximately 500,000 years ago. Extensive excavations nearby have unearthed the remains of Upper Cave Man (Homo sapiens), who dwelt there some 18,000 years ago. The Chinese government has erected an excellent exhibition hall on the site with specimens, pictures and the story of the evolution of man, his life styles, tools, use of fire and his gradual development, both physically and as a social being.

In the last fifteen years, I have visited over fifty cities and towns in China and each place has a story to tell. My three thousand slides and scores of snapshots each record an incident, person or memorable event, too numerous to mention.

One other aspect of China that has fascinated me is the fact that there exists in the country fifty-five nationalities, other than the Han people who make up ninety-four percent of the population. Nationalities and costumes have always intrigued me. I have a collection of over 150 dolls in their national costumes from all over the world, including a number of the minority peoples of China. These minorities are widely scattered, and the number in each group varies from 100,000 to 10,000,000. It is impossible to visit them all, but I have been able to meet seven or eight of the minorities in the course of my travels.

The rolling, treeless steppes of Inner Mongolia are home to a roving people who, moving with their herds, disinclined to settle in permanent homes. Even as they migrate, they must protect themselves against a winter which often begins in September and may not be frost-free until the end of June or early July. The people who live in this area are descendants of the race who conquered China under Ghengis and Kublai Khan and retreated to this northern area after the Mongols were driven out of China proper. Their music and dance speak of vast blue skies, moonlight on the wide prairies, love, and the fun of riding, rodeos and fairs. After the southern cities, I found Mongolia a great relief from the crowds and traffic jams.

On one occasion, I wandered on my own to a small settlement and was met by a friendly soul who greeted me with smiles revealing a mouth of gold-covered teeth. Though neither of us spoke a common language, communication was instant. I was invited in to her house and was introduced to her cat sitting on the k'ang — the long shelf on which the family sleep and eat and under which a fire burns most of the year to keep everyone warm.

Having inspected the house, I was taken out to see her chickens in their mud-brick coop, and then introduced to her daughter, son-in-law and grandson. As we "talked," a herdsman rode by with a vast herd of sheep and goats bound for a grassy hillside. What a restful change from Beijing's six million bicycles, thousands of heavily loaded trucks, buses, taxis and its ten million inhabitants.

The following day, we visited a yurt and I tasted the most delicious yogurt I have ever had. Dining on milk, tea and Mongolian tidbits, while sitting on a k'ang and being entertained with songs by a herdsman's daughter, was an experience not to be forgotten. I tried my hand at a bow and arrow and had a ride on a Bactrian camel, the two-humped "ship of the desert." As I regretfully left the grasslands commune, I was presented with a male and female costume of the Mongolian people, which I prize along with costumes from several other areas.

Travelling over the trackless steppes and then through the mountains, we reached Huhhot, capital of Inner Mongolia. There our group visited the Artists School and we were entertained by a male instrumentalist in a brilliant turquoise costume, an attractive female vocalist, and four young women in multi-coloured dresses performing a beautiful rainbow dance. Mongolian entertainers are among the best. I would like to have booked them then and there for a tour across Canada.

A visit to a nationalities factory revealed the products of the area. Here were the leather saddles and belts, the fur jackets and caps, the silver-handled knives carried in the rider's belt and the most splendid array of leather boots. I chose for myself a pair of cream leather boots appliqued with red and blue designs, and after eight years of wear, they are still as comfortable and presentable as they ever were.

Further to the north-west I met the Uigher people, formerly nomads, who roamed the area in the early days, but now have settled down as farmers and tradesmen, developing their own written language and books. Today they are often leaders in their communities. The mayor of Urumqi, the capital city of Xinjiang province, is a Uigher. They have adapted to the desert areas, cultivating large vineyards on the oases of the Turpan depression and building amazing underground water tunnels from the distant mountains to irrigate their crops. They are a mixed nationality with Mongolian and Turkish strains, and like all the nationalities of China, have produced their own art, music and culture.

One of the most fascinating places I visited was the Turpan bazaar. Outside our motel-style inn, two little boys were waiting for likely customers. Three of us agreed to be conveyed there on a donkey cart consisting of planks laid across two sets of wheels harnessed to one of my favourite animals, the placid little Chinese donkey. In the market there was everything from pots and pans, boots, dresses, dry goods, beautiful embroideries, unique little square Uigher hats, to lamb shish-kebabs and the delicious Turpan spiced bread (thrown like a pancake against the inside of an open round oven and baked to a golden brown). I bought two beautiful pieces of embroidery, two Uigher hats and a dress length of the local patterned material which I later had made up into a Uigher dress. In the course of our shopping we were, of course, followed by curious townsfolk. We made friends with numerous small boys with curly feathers in their caps and little girls in their Uigher dresses.

Turpan was one of the stopping points on the Silk Road. Nearby are deserted cities which were once thriving stopovers, where merchants could make the final preparations for the hazardous trip across the remaining miles of desert and through the snow-capped mountains to Europe.

The desolate area between Turpan and the city of Urumqi was like a moonscape. On the "mountains of fire" burning red in the sunset, temperatures rose to 160 degrees farenheit in the summer, but it was this dry heat that preserved one of China's great treasures, the Dunhuang Caves. A detour of a few short miles off the Silk Road led the caravans of the Middle Ages to four hundred caves, known as the Mogao Grottoes, decorated by devout patrons of the arts with frescoes, paintings, carvings and sculptures honouring Buddha or depicting the life of the day. Here the travelers prayed for safety from robbers, the mountain cold, sandstorms, and all other ills besetting them on their journey eastward. During a period of civil war some centuries later, devout priests covered and disguised the caves which were not rediscovered and restored until the nineteenth century.

A visit through the caves gives a picture of Buddhist art from the Eastern Jin through the Sui, T'ang, Five dynasties, Song and Yuan dynasties — nearly a thousand years of art, history and culture.

Many of the murals and statues illustrate the life of Sakyamuni, the Nepalese prince, who gave up his noble birthright to be a humble monk, a seeker after truth, eventually becomming the revered Buddha of the religion that bears his name. Groups of officials, emperors, and merchants from other countries in their native dress are shown discoursing with Buddhist teachers. Graceful flying musicians or "angels" often hover over the scenes.

One drawing, which never appears in any descriptive booklet of the grottoes tickled our fancy. An artist, obviously bored with the themes of the paintings, introduced his own little humorous touch. Tucked in the corner of one large fresco was a half circle of hissing cats, their claws raised against an opposing half circle of dogs, fangs bared, and obviously growling menacingly. Meanwhile, in a complete cirle around them sat a row of monkeys laughing their heads off. Unfortunately one cannot take pictures in the caves and no postcards are ever produced to show this scene.

As one moves further to the northwest, to Urumqi, the farthest inland city in the world, one meets the Kazak people, the "cowboys" of China. They number about one million, and, like the Uighers, they were nomads who roamed from the Caspian Sea to the northern steppes. Many of them have relatives in Russia, as man- made borders do not separate their wide-ranging communities. They are expert horsemen, born to the saddle, and have bred horses for centuries. Now cattle, sheep and goats make their area an important centre of husbandry. They remain partially nomadic although they are settling into communities at least for the winter. Community get-togethers consist of horse racing and games played on horseback. Even courting is done on horseback. If a young man rides after the girl of his choice and she returns on her horse alone, he is spurned; if they ride back together all is well.

We came across a large gathering of Kazaks on our way to Celestial Lake. They had come together for a meeting and many of their yurts had been erected on the hillside beside the road we were travelling. We stopped to make friends. Unused to contact with foreigners, some of them shyly retreated, but we were invited by others into their tents and saw the beautiful hand-woven carpets, the embroidered clothes and the woollen blankets they had produced.

Most of the minority people live in mountainous areas or parts of the country impossible to visit because of lack of transportation, roads, hotels, and conveniences considered necessary for foreign visitors. However, Yunnan province, which is home to many of the minority nationalities, is accessible in many parts. Here we met the Sani people, who live on the edge of the Stone Forest. About 120 kilometres from Kunming, the capital of Yunnan, is some of the most fantastic scenery of China, a limestone "forest" of slender pinnacles, eroded by rainwater to produce unique shapes. One's imagination runs wild with the strange contours and figures created by nature, and it is not difficult to see how "elephant rock," or "alligator crag" get their names. The "kissing chickens" tickled my fancy, and the "fairy's home," with its flat rock bed and round table was the setting for a local folk tale.

Walking through the defiles and climbing up the paths one meets more strange and beautiful sights. A huge rock that appears ready to fall at any moment may momentarily deter one from proceeding, but the guide insists that it is guaranteed not to fail for the next ten thousand years. Sword Peak Pool is a jewel in a natural setting. A sharp stone blade thrusts up out of the crystal water, as fish glide in and out of the shadows cast by the reflections of sky and rocks. Silhouetted against the sky stands a little pagoda on a pinnacle.

On the outskirts of this "forest" lie the villages of the Sani people, a tribe of the Yi nationality, the fourth largest in China with four to five million people. The Yi are an agricultural people who live largely in an environment of rocky slopes and rolling plateaus. The Sani have adapted to the large number of visitors who come to their area, and when groups visit, the Sani present a programme of songs and dances that is most entertaining. Their numbers range from dances depicting their everyday work to an amusing presentation of wrestling with a wily tiger. Musical instruments are chiefly home-made but provide excellent background for their entertainment. The women's beautifully embroidered jackets and hand-made embroidered shoes with turned-up toes, add colour and interest to a festive evening. I never cease to marvel at their energy. They work in the fields all day, then sing and dance for two hours in the evening, yet when they invite us to join them in a dance at the end of the programme we are exhausted after ten minutes.

Leaving Kunming by air we travelled for an hour further to the southwest into an area known as Xishuangbanna, the subtropical home of many of the twenty-four minority nationalities that live in Yunnan. A five-hour bus ride took us to Jinghong, the area inhabited by the Tai people, originally from Thailand but for generations Chinese citizens. They are a warm, friendly people and maintain a distinct culture akin to the home from which they originally came.

One of the most memorable visits I have ever made in China was to a Tai village in the hills near the city of Menghai. We were received with such warmth and affection that, hours later when we left, it was almost a tearful parting. The whole village came out to greet us and then invited us to come to the top of the hill where their temple and pagoda were situated. One of our group, who wasn't able to do much climbing, was reluctant to go. But one of the women put her arm around her and slowly and gently helped her up to the top. When they sat down on a bench to rest, our member gave her assistant a kiss, and there began a five- minute "love-in" of hugging and kissing.

A sixty-year-old woman, (I mentally called her mamma-boss) organized all the teenage girls to dance for us, and then had us join the dance as it circled the magnificent pagoda. The four colourful corner towers and the tall central pinnacle rising thirty feet into the soft warm air of the hilltop, were beautiful beyond description. As we danced, we spied a number of little shaven-headed, orange-clad young boys whom we discovered were students at a Buddhist school that stood beside the pagoda. They were dressed like little monks but were not novices and were free to leave when their schooling was completed. Attached to their school was the village thatch-covered temple, with its large Buddha and altar.

When festivities were over, we all — villagers and visitors — trooped down the hill again and reluctantly said farewell. It was a memorable day.

Back in Jinghong, we went to the park to see the green peacocks for which the area is famous, and I picked up on a street stall a sarong with the printed design of the peacock's eye and feathers. Within a day I was able to have the short-waisted blouse made to match the colour of the sarong, and to complete the outfit I purchased a beautiful silver belt which held the sarong in place. All the women of this area wore the ankle length sarong typical of South-East Asia.

Arrangements were made for us to have a Tai meal in a private home. To our astonishment, a woman and her husband prepared and served our group and guides with only a tripod over an open fire and a two-hole stove into which the steamers were sunk. We sat on the floor, around four tiny tables each serving eight, and thoroughly enjoyed the delicious food and the rice steamed in long pieces of split bamboo.

The following day, our guide promised us an unusual trip and we set off expectantly. To call it unusual was an understatement, but it was great fun. We arrived at a river's edge and he informed us that we were to visit a Hani village across the river.

"Take off your shoes and socks," he ordered, when flat bamboo rafts arrived. Standing on these six-foot wide rafts, holding hands to keep ourselves steady, we pulled ourselves across the river by a taut guiding rope strung from shore to shore. One or two nervous souls preferred to remain behind, but actually the water was very shallow and the current sluggish. Most of us enjoyed the novel method of travel and were glad of the opportunity to visit the rather shy Hani people in this isolated village.

Two other nationalities I have met only casually, are the Korean and Tibetan people.

In northeast China, many Koreans have settled in the provinces bordering their country. I have been in Korea on several occasions and admire these charming and industrious people, but I have never had the opportunity of visiting their villages in China. We did, however, meet a friendly group of Korean women from North China on the Great Wall and had our pictures taken with them. Their distinctive dress readily identifies them wherever they are.

Visitors from the autonomous area of Tibet — for centuries a vassal of China — are quite often seen travelling, particularly in the southwest. They have access to this part of the country by air from Lhasa to Chengdu. Again, their distinctive dress, as well as their somewhat darker skin, single them out.

I also met some Tibetan monks in Lanzhou, and they were so eager to have their pictures taken that they stood in front of our cameras for as long as we would take snapshots.

The minority groups of China vary greatly in size. Fifteen of them have a population of over one million, while the smallest group, the Hezhes, have less than two thousand people. Although the total number represents a very small portion of the country's population, they are scattered over sixty percent of China's land mass. Many of them still wear their traditional dress, which is part of their culture and relates to their history and environment. A study of costume gives insight into their lifestyle and background.

Mary Seddon, in her recent book entitled *National Minority Costume in China* says:

> The women of China's minority people display their intelligence and ability through their costume. For instance, women from the southern minority groups are responsible for the whole process of costume design — from the growing and harvesting of the cotton to its spinning, weaving, wax-dyeing, embroidery and tailoring. It can take up to several years to produce a really exquisite costume. Women also attempt to convey their feelings and dreams through the designing of their costumes. The motifs of their design include flowers, birds and animals, the actual interpretation of which is influenced by their particular knowledge and experience. These motifs thus transcend into an art form.

> . . . . Although the actual material of the costumes is not particularly valuable, the finished product can be very colourful and glamorous. The skills which have been passed down from generation to generation have enabled the costumes to gradually evolve into virtual works of art with a high aesthetic value.

China's recent development of a fashion industry has sparked an interest in the ethnic costumes of her minority people. The fashion show, presented at the Pacific National Exhibition in Vancouver in 1988, and then on to other centres including Paris, was hailed as a resounding success. It was obvious that some of the clothes had strong national overtones, adapted cleverly to modern design. In this regard, some of the clothing experts in China are re-examining their own fashion roots. Kunming, the capital of a province with twenty-four different minority groups is emerging as an innovative fashion centre. A recent article entitled "Ethnic Costumes Inspire New Fashions" in the June 1989 edition of the magazine *China Reconstructs*, illustrates the new clothes based on original minority costumes. A fashion show presenting two hundred new designs to the public was received with enthusiasm and excitement.

The minority people, with their long history and distinctive culture, have much to contribute to China. The freedom to conduct their schools in their own languages for the first few years, and the building of institutes of higher learning to encourage the study and development of the rich contribution these diverse groups have to offer, should enrich the cultural life of a developing nation.

Conclusion

China's story is an ongoing saga. Over my lifetime, the scenarios have changed rapidly. I have seen a proud and intransigent imperial dynasty overthrown, the unsuccessful struggle of a republic to maintain control and finally the domination of the Communist regime. To see so much change in eighty years, and, for some of that time, to have been part of it, has been for me an extraordinary experience. After I saw the film *The Last Emperor*, I came out of the theatre in a daze. I felt as though I had lived my life all over again. I was born the year the Little Emperor, Pu Yi, came to the throne, and I had lived through many of the events depicted in the film. It was a strange and moving experience.

For a country with a 5,000-year history, such overwhelming changes in so short a time are traumatic. Each generation is faced with a new challenge, a changing society, shifting goals and rules of conduct. The generation gap becomes a yawning chasm. The girls I taught in the thirties were disturbed by the changing mores and the fact that their parents could not identify with their aims and desires. Now, into the nineties, young people are demanding rights and liberties never dreamed of by the previous generation. Authorities are unable to make changes fast enough for the youth, with the consequent unrest and turmoil.

Meanwhile China is struggling to take her place among the great nations of the world in the twenty-first century. As the countries of the

Pacific Rim come more and more into the international picture, Canada — as a member of this community — cannot afford to neglect her relationship with the restless giant that is China. Whatever we may think about the Chinese form of government, it is essential we remember that friendship is a bond that creates trust and understanding. If and when China moves to a more democratic form of government, it must be created by China to suit her needs, not a carbon copy imposed by a foreign power.

Because I believe in friendship, I have spent the last ten years of my life deeply engaged in the work of the Federation of Canada-China Friendship Associations. When I accepted the position of Tour Director, it was with the strong conviction that, by taking people to China and introducing them to people in communes and urban centres, in schools and churches, in factories and community enterprises, I was helping to build bridges of friendship that would in a small way contribute to understanding and world peace.

Lately, as national president of the Federation, I have become aware of the tremendous outpouring of friendship that the local associations have expended on the Chinese students and scholars studying in Canada in recent years. Many of these students have become such good friends, that we treasure opportunities to see them again when we visit China. Such personal contacts withstand political turmoil and help to cement a bond between two countries that share a place in the Pacific Rim and in the wider community of nations.

Another bond between Canada and China is the legacy of Dr. Norman Bethune. November 12, 1989, marked the fiftieth anniversary of his death in active service with the Liberation Army in North China. March 3, 1990, marked the one hundredth anniversary of his birth. These two events were celebrated on November 11 and 13, 1989, in Beijing and Shijiazhuang, the site of the Peace Memorial Hospital and the grave of Dr. Bethune. It was my privilege to lead a small delegation to represent Canada at the celebrations in both cities and to address the audience of 3,000 in the Great Hall of the People in Beijing.

In Shijiazhuang, a memorial service was held in the hospital, and wreaths from thirty-five different organizations and government departments were laid on his grave. A new wing of the Bethune museum was opened, with displays of calligraphy and children's art focusing on the Canada-China relationship and Dr. Bethune's contribution. The memory of Dr. Bethune's service to China is kept alive in the minds of the people by such ceremonies. Without doubt, other Canadians, notably Dr. Robert McClure, contributed as much or more to China's struggle and survival, but Bethune became a symbol of hope and an inspiration at a crucial time. His daring exploits became a legend woven into the fabric of China's revolutionary struggle.

It is my hope that my experiences with the "three Chinas" of the twentieth century will give Canadians a better understanding of this land which has opened its doors to us in recent years. For much of her long and illustrious history, China has been isolated and relatively unknown. Now for her to achieve a place in the global community is a monumental task which requires our cooperation and understanding. It also requires recognition, on the part of China's leaders, that they must satisfy the needs and longings of their people in a peaceful and humane way. The last decade of the twentieth century is crucial to China's emergence as a credible and stable democratic world power.

Bibliography

Alley, Rewi. *Rewi Alley on Gung Ho.* Beijing: Peking Review Press, 1989.

Hunter, Deidre and Neale (ed.) *We the Chinese. Voices from Asia.* New York: Praeger Publishers, 1971.

Leland, Charles G. *Pidgin-English Sing-Song.* London: Kegan, Paul, Trench, Tribune and Co. Ltd., 1904.

Lewis, C.E.(ed.) *Poems Worth Knowing.* Vancouver: Copp Clark Publishing Co Ltd., 1941.

Scott, Munroe. *McLure, The China Years.* Toronto: Canec Publishing and Supply House, 1977.

Seddon, Mary. *National Minority Costumes in China.* Hong Kong: Joint Publishing Co., 1985.

Snow, Edgar. *Red Star Over China.* New York: Random House, 1944.